Old English Poems and Riddles

CHRIS MCCULLY is a writer and teacher based in Groningen, in the north of the Netherlands, where he has lived since 2003. Educated at the universities of Newcastle-upon-Tyne and Manchester, for many years Chris worked in what was the Department of English Language and Literature at Manchester, specialising in English phonology, English metrics, and the history of the English language. His many previous publications span research papers, textbooks, works on fly-fishing, criticism, literary essays and reviews, and a memoir on alcoholism and recovery, together with three collections of verse published by Carcanet: *Time Signatures* (1993), *Not Only I* (1996) and *The Country of Perhaps* (2006).

T0096552

Fyfield*Books* aim to make available some of the great classics of British and European literature in clear, affordable formats, and to restore often neglected writers to their place in literary tradition.

Fyfield*Books* take their name from the Fyfield elm in Matthew Arnold's 'Scholar Gypsy' and 'Thyrsis'. The tree stood not far from the village where the series was originally devised in 1971.

> *Roam on! The light we sought is shining still.*
> *Dost thou ask proof? Our tree yet crowns the hill,*
> *Our Scholar travels yet the loved hill-side*

from 'Thyrsis'

Old English Poems and Riddles

Translated with an introduction by
CHRIS McCULLY

Fyfield*Books*
CARCANET

First published in Great Britain in 2008 by
Carcanet Press Limited
Alliance House
Cross Street
Manchester M2 7AQ

A CIP catalogue record for this book is available from the British Library
ISBN 978 1 85754 925 6

The publisher acknowledges financial assistance from
Arts Council England

Typeset by XL Publishing Services, Tiverton
Printed and bound in England by SRP Ltd, Exeter

This work is dedicated to the memory of
Steve Glosecki, 1952–2007

Contents

Introduction

I've lived with these poems for most of my adult life. Fortunately or unfortunately I have usually, and until quite recently, responded to them with instincts that properly belong to a philologist. Those instincts were sharpened by an enduring professional interest in metrical matters, but that is no excuse.

It was coincidentally in Greenland that this long-developed, even ingrained, pedantry was challenged. During September 2004 I spent some time alone in a remote part of Greenland. Ostensibly there in order to catch Arctic charr with the fly-rod and to write a couple of feature articles, I also took along an old student edition of C.L. Wrenn's *Beowulf*. (In paperback, this was lighter to carry in the rucksack than, say, Klaeber, whose edition I would otherwise have preferred.) 'Read the thing as a *poem*, Chris,' I thought, 'not just as an unhappy hunting-ground for unhappy metrists.'

And so each night I would re-read *Beowulf*, trying not to be distracted by my small knowledge of the poem's analogues, the purpose (if any) of its digressions, its propensity for recapitulation, the presence of ancient sound-changes and the mystery of its occasional hypermetric lines.

Sometimes, at some unearthly hour of the morning, an Arctic fox would bark, somewhere outside the tent. The dawn would be full of strange shufflings, the sound of the stress of the wind. I hunched into a sleeping-bag and went back to the poem, lost in its landscape of failure and shadows. I read by torchlight. There was no other human being for a hundred square miles. The monsters were real.

*

The result of that encounter was a poem of my own ('After Beowulf', published a year later in *PN Review*), which I wrote in a version of the great two-part Anglo-Saxon line. The time-frame supporting that poem was the endless moment just after Beowulf's extinction on his funeral pyre – an eternity of uselessness in which his people, the Geats, are suspended by the poet at the end of the poem. The gold? Useless. The dragon-slaying? Pointless. The earlier triumphs and the getting of renown? Useless. All the busyness and activity of the poem itself? Useless. The poet's comment, as Beowulf's mortal remains are torched, is merely 'Heaven swallowed the smoke.' I responded to the laconic almost as much as to the sadness.

1

These reading encounters were at least partly encounters with the development of my own technique. The philologist somehow rejoined the reader nearly thirty years after the two had been divorced. Then both met the writer I had become. It was a matter of assurance, and of trust.

These are metrical translations. I need to say something about that.

Long ago I'd wanted Old English verse to be what J.C. Pope and a handful of others (indeed, some very distinguished others) had wished it to be, namely the kind of isochronic structure that could go to a tune, punctuated (or not) by the strokes of a harp. The term 'isochrony' needs a gloss. By it, I mean that Pope and others develop a system by which Old English verse may be performed in terms of measures analogous to the bars of later Western music, where each beat (which usually falls on a linguistic stress) of each half-line ushers in a measure which extends over all subsequent linguistic material up to, but not including, the next beat (usually another linguistic stress). So in the half-line *lange hwīle* ('a long while', *Beowulf*, 16a), Pope and others might claim that there were two measures, the first beginning with the stressed syllable *lan(ge)*, the second beginning with the stressed syllable of *hwī(le)*. Pope and others have also claimed that such bars have necessarily equivalent structures; that there are two bars to each half-line; and that silent beats (analogous to structural musical rests) can be accommodated within the underlying structure.

In order to support this view I had looked, as my illustrious predecessors had looked, for philological and other evidence: the use of the word *song*, the descriptions of poetry and poets; back then to Tacitus, and his descriptions of the verse-making habits of the Germanic tribes; and then to linguistics, and the form of the syllables themselves, the likelihood of the stressed syllables occurring isochronically… And so on – and on. In truth, my first serious research into *Beowulf* (I was a beginning graduate, it was 1982) involved making a set of phonemic transcriptions, although how I thought I could describe the underlying structure of – presumably – West Saxon in this way, and do so in transcriptions that were also phonologically faithful to the language of the time, is now quite beyond me. Then I would match each transcription to a Pope-style temporal score (though in three-measure bars rather than in the four-four time of Pope); detail how the same half-line appeared in Sievers as a Type; cross-check the Sieversian ascription against Bliss's later catalogue…

I still have those notes somewhere. Heaven shall swallow the smoke.

I think I was wrong. I think Heusler and Pope were wrong, that Creed was wrong, that Obst is wrong. I no longer think Old English alliterative verse goes to a tune, or ever could. I even suspect that the language itself, back in that very long stretch of time when Germanic alliterative verse was composed and enjoyed, did not have the same kind of underlying rhythmic structure as present-day English. (I would myself wish to argue that it was less stress-timed, contrary to the assumptions of almost the entire critical community.) We do not know what the harp was for, can't reconstruct how this material was performed. We don't know much about its audience. Pity.

I prefer the less glamorous view that Old English verse is – like its analogues in Continental Europe, like the Norse verse of the Edda – a kind of aural architecture. Tolkien's comment, made in an aside in his fine essay about *Beowulf*, was that such verse is 'more like masonry than music'.

If the verse, or at least the 'classical' verse composed or collected during the cultural greatness that begins in seventh-century Northumbria and lasts to around the second decade of the eleventh century, is a kind of aural architecture, then how is the architecture arrived at?

If students of Old English have studied this topic at all they might have learnt something about Sievers' Five Types. Sievers' essays on the Types appeared most famously in 1885. Those who have been exposed to 'the Five Types' know that in Sievers' terms each half-line may be described, more or less comfortably, as belonging to one of five main variant patterns, labelled A (the commonest type of half-line, crudely / x…/ x, where '…' means 'this part of the half-line can be expanded across up to four unstressed syllables') through B (x…/ x /), C (x…/ / x), D (/ / \ x, / / x \, or more rarely / x / \ x) and E (/ \ x /).

Sievers' work is very great, but I do not think it is quite right (for reasons I have explored several times, and published elsewhere). My hunch as to the non-rightness of Sievers then encountered some of the insights of what linguists call Optimality Theory (OT), and in that context I learnt much about metrical structures from the work of Bruce Hayes, whose development of OT to encompass metrics was, and is, the clearest statement I know of how metrical closure interacts with other constraints on structure which, in concert, help to generate a well-structured (half-)line. The term 'well-structured' again requires a gloss. By it, I mean those half-lines which are attested as occurring – and usually, as multiply-occurring. Ill-structured half-lines – such as the almost-possible but everywhere non-occurring 'xxxxx / xxxxx /' – are non-occurring precisely because they seem to violate some principle of construction whose existence it is the task of the analyst to deduce from the available evidence. At the same time, I was also greatly attracted by Tom Cable's restatement of the structure of the Old English half-line as a mapping of linguistic material into four abstract *positions*.

It was out of that conceptual mess of preoccupations that I first started to fiddle about with a version of the half-line which was, precisely, a mapping of linguistic material into four positions, but with inviolable constraints on how each half-line could end, and with a further constraint which in principle allowed the opening of each metrical unit – each half-line, thus – to be relatively free. (As Hayes has put it, 'Beginnings free, endings strict'.) That also helped me to understand how hypermetric lines come about: in my current view these extra-long variant lines have absolutely free openings, but position 4, the last slot in the half-line, must be very strictly filled, something that impacts in turn on how position 3 may be filled. This gives the *effect* of metricality but at the same time allows the poet great thematic freedom together with a chance for virtuoso display. An example is

þurhdrīfan hī mē mid deorcan næglum
… 'free' opening.................. (3)   4

'they drove dark nails through me'
('The Dream of the Rood', 46a)*

(Alliteration on the /d/ of *þurhdrīfan* is on this view merely decorative.)

Such a view had the added advantage that I could include what A.J. Bliss called 'light verses' into the structure. By 'light verses' Bliss did not of course mean verses of the form 'There once was a young man called Grendel...' He meant half-lines which had the requisite four positions of structure, each filled prototypically by one or more syllables, but which had only one major stress. Such half-lines, which occur frequently in the corpus, pose a severe if not insuperable problem to the isochronically minded. To a translator,

---

* The written symbol þ is pronounced 'th' as in '**th**rough'; the macron over vowel shapes such as ī and ē is a length-mark, and indicates that the vowel is pronounced long; æ is pronounced roughly as the 'a' in 'hat', and the 'g' of 'næglum' is pronounced rather as 'y' ('nay-lum'). The symbol ð (see e.g. p. 12) is pronounced 'th' as in '**th**en'.

though, the presence of such half-lines is a relief just as much as it a challenge, since he is not constrained to fill each half-line of his metrical translations with what are by-and-large-but-with-some-exceptions two thumps of stress per half-line. No. The original material is far more refined, varied, and skilfully deployed than that.

*

The four-position view of the structure of OE half-lines can be illustrated by the following example. The line *gomban gyldan; þæt wæs gōd cyning* occurs early in *Beowulf* (line 11). It consists of two half-lines, the first *gomban gyldan* ('to give tribute'), the second *þæt wæs gōd cyning* ('he was a good king'). The first half-line, *gomban gyldan*, has exactly four syllables, each of which fills exactly one abstract metrical position:

Positions	1	2	3	4
	gom	ban	gyl	dan

The second half-line, *þæt wæs gōd cyning*, contains five syllables, the first two of which, and the last of which, are unstressed. The first two unstressed syllables fill the position 1 slot, while the rest of the linguistic material is matched with the remaining positions:

Positions	1	2	3	4
	þæt wæs	gōd	cy	ning

*

It would be wrong for me to claim total metrical correspondence between the half-lines of the originals and the half-lines I have deployed in the translations. Where an Anglo-Saxon poet has chosen to structure a given half-line as, say, an A or a D Type (to use Sievers' terminology) I have not necessarily felt constrained to translate that same chunk of language as an A or a D. What I have done is to try and translate the poems using a selection of rhythmical and metrical patterns *equivalent* to those available to poets writing in Old English. Even then, there are uncomfortably many places in the translations where the alert reader will find patterns in present-day English that could never have been available to an Anglo-Saxon poet. An instance is 'in the gaunt earth's depth' ('The Wanderer', line 84). A present-day reader would perhaps put more relative stress on *earth's* than on *gaunt*, and indeed the chief phrasal stress of that half-line lies on the final word, *depth*. Because of the phrasal stress of present-day English, then, the half-line reads as a sequence of five syllables, the final four of which participate in a rising, a gradient pattern of stress. Such a gradient pattern was not available to a poet composing in Old English (or, more cautiously, if that pattern *was* available, no Old English poet seems to have deployed it in verse). It's true that I have tweaked the half-line, and allowed it to alliterate on /g/ (*graved his gold-friend in the gaunt earth's depth*), implying that the syllables *gaunt* and *depth* are relatively more stressed than *earth's*. That would be merely a possible rhythmic reading in present-day English, but I stress (apologies) that such a structure wouldn't necessarily have been available to a poet 1000 years ago, and that therefore my work is a set of compromises, or adjustments. *Absolute* fidelity was impossible for me. I suspect it would be for any poet, however talented.

Another feature of the originals which I was sometimes unable – more often, unwilling – to reproduce was what metrists call 'suspension of resolution'. In those same originals, and within the same metrical foot, two syllables, the first of which is short and stressed, may under some circumstances count as equivalent to one long stressed syllable. Thus, for example, the first two syllables of the verb *fremedon*, 'they performed', count metrically as if they spanned just one metrical position. Accordingly, although the half-line *ellen fremedon* (*Beowulf*, 3b: 'they performed valorous deeds') has five syllables, those five syllables occupy only four metrical slots: *el-* (1), *-len* (2), *freme-* (3), *-don* (4).

The problem is that in the originals, resolution is sometimes suspended, and it's characteristically suspended in a specific circumstance, namely, when the syllable preceding the potentially resolvable sequence is itself heavy (i.e. contains a long vowel, or a short vowel followed by two or more consonants). Under this principle – which Russom, Fulk, Cable and other great scholars have made clear – a half-line such as *þēod-cyninga* (*Beowulf*, 2a: 'of the peoples' kings') has four syllables, but the first two syllables of *cyninga*, which would otherwise match the general criteria for resolution, are not (or at least, arguably are not) resolved, since the syllable which precedes them, *þēod-*, is heavy.

This rule – if it is a rule – interests me very much, because it seems to exist only on the page. I doubt any pre-literate *scop* ('scop', pronounced with an initial 'sh', is the Old English term for the poet, and is related to the verb *to shape*) would or could ever have been aware of such a rule, and indeed the existence of such a principle seems to confirm the truism that whatever its oral origins, the Old English verse which has survived has a highly scriptist bias.

Purists, therefore, will shake their heads over these translations, where I have sometimes allowed resolution to be suspended in ways an Anglo-Saxon scribe might have understood, but where sometimes I have ignored all scriptism, and all good philology, in the name of getting the verse, including even an approximation of the relevant metrics, to work at all as verse.

*

There are other places where I found myself unwilling (less frequently, unable) to constrain a half-line strictly to four positions. That is to say, the reader will find a relatively higher proportion of the Type Sievers called D* (/ x / \ x) in some of these translations than he or she might expect to find in the original Old English, and he or she will similarly find more examples of B Types where I have allowed *both* the unstressed positions to be expanded (rather than the *one* it would be routinely possible to expand in classically constructed Old English verse). Generally, though, where I have allowed myself the last licence I have also, usually (but again, not always), made sure that one of the expanded unstressed positions has contained prefixes, which seem to be exempt from normative metrical constraints in the originals (something that Russom was the first to point out, brilliantly). There, at least, I was working with principles I think a *scop* would have endorsed – although possibly that same *scop* would here and there have been critical of my basic metrical techniques.

What no *scop* would ever have endorsed is the freedom with which I have allowed the half-lines to alliterate. Old English verse commonly (although not invariably) alliterated in an 'aa:ax' pattern – two alliterating, primarily stressed syllables in the first half-line, and only one in the second, with the last stressed syllable of the entire line rarely, if ever, participating in the alliterative pattern for that line. (This common patterning is the absolute rule in the late poem, 'Durham'.) An example is the line

...**g**omban **g**yldan; þæt wæs **g**ōd cyning (*Beowulf*, 11)
  a   a   a   x

'...to give tribute; he was a good king'

(The line alliterates on /g/; the /k(y)/ of *cyning* does not alliterate, since that syllable can only rarely participate in the alliterative pattern binding the two half-lines together.)

The chief problem for the translator is that if one constructs lines such as 'Bitter the battle-rush; bale was horrible...' then the alliterating /b/ sounds, these days, simply too overt – or perhaps, again, I'm saying no more than it sounds pretty /b/loody terrible to my ear. I venture, however, that I would have wearied the aurally sensitive reader if I had filled every line with the classical alliterative pattern. And so I have varied it – sometimes using crossed alliteration, sometimes transverse; sometimes using one alliterating syllable in the first half-line, sometimes allowing the last stressed syllable of the line to chime with syllables picked out for stress in the first half-line. In a word, I sought freedom – although it was a very limited freedom. Further, where I found that the original also, because of tactical astuteness, or simply because of incompetence, made use of similar variety, I sighed gratefully, and took a mile, since (I thought) the original had implicitly asked me to take an inch.

Another structure the alert reader will find different from the original is that found in the so-called hypermetric half-lines. There are relatively few of these extra-long lines in the Anglo-Saxon corpus, though they occur with strange regularity in 'The Dream of the Rood' and in 'Genesis B' (which last is not translated here). For all the earnest ink that has been expended on their structure, no scholar knows why these lines should be extra-long, or what their aesthetic purpose might have been (a slowing of narrative pace? thematic emphasis? virtuoso metrical display?).

If I temporarily wear my long-abandoned scholar's hat I would tell you that in my view these apparently anomalous lines are actually quite *regular*: they are examples of the metrical constraint 'Beginnings free, endings strict'. To that extent, and as I've hinted above, they seem to have totally free openings (that is, positions 1 and 2 may be filled completely freely) – and yet they have, always, very strict closures. (Notably, too, if position 4 is strictly filled, this has a consequence for the type of linguistic material that can fill position 3, so metrical freedom is constrained to occur only in positions 1 and 2.) Furthermore, the second of two adjacent hypermetric half-lines (where these occur in the same long line) has usually a somewhat lighter and tighter structure than the first. If I were to lineate such structures in a properly scholarly edition, rather than a book of translations, I would follow the great editors. Yet in the present text I have, I'm afraid, lineated in such a way that the *second* of the two adjacent hypermetric half-lines itself contains what look like two half-lines. It was, primarily, a matter of end-focus, and of typography. The present lineation does not quite capture my current technical understanding of the metrics behind such hypermetric lines, but it was the best compromise I could reach here.

I say I fiddled about. I had done similar fiddling at several points in a dubious past. For instance, while still a very young man I had written many pastiches of Old English verse, including some that were structurally (i.e. metrically, and in terms of diction) relatively accurate. I had even written (worse, published) in Old English – if I remember correctly, one full-blown elegy (some nonsense about a ship that laments its way through its own burial), and reconstructed the lost beginning to the poem that history has come to know as 'The Battle of Maldon'. I had also written – I can hardly call them 'poems' – in present-day English but had used the ancient alliterative form as the poem was emerging from its junctures of ambition and wrong-headedness. One or two of these efforts even won prizes. The prizes had the disastrous effect of encouraging me, at least for a while.

I had, as it were, a kind of Form. It's probably worth repeating that my interests in this kind of verse did not arise from reading, say, Pound's pastiche of 'The Seafarer', or even Auden's pastiches and imitations of Old English (none of which are particularly accurate... but there speaks the pedant again). Rather, they can be likened to the preoccupations of an amateur car mechanic who is trying to fix the engine (and – why not? – the bodywork) of the heap of history, rust and hopelessness he calls his car. Pretty, aesthetic, cultured he is not, this man. He is merely dirty, oily-overalled and persistent. There are weird bits of the wreck – stray pieces of metal, unlovely corrosions – which will not fit back into their rightful places. There are also some left-over parts whose original purpose is utterly mysterious. Still, after plenty of swearing, and some indiscriminate banging and tweaking, the wreck runs. The fact that it runs at all is a minor miracle.

*

In the end I have merely tried to make the poems as attractive to readers as they are to me. After all, one of the things that impressed me when I began to study these poems was their sheer variety. It impresses me still. Alongside the elegies there are gnomic verses, epics, riddles, pieces of versified hagiography, bits of travel writing, valedictions, charms, pieces that have been commissioned and pieces that seem to have been written for no reason at all.

I tried to represent some (though not all) of that variety, particularly in a reading context where many people – often, kind and even educated people – seem to think that Old English literature consists of Seamus Heaney's translation of *Beowulf* and what one student once memorably described as 'Pond's Seafarer'.

It would be most unwise to use these translations as a crib. I have been, sometimes, fussily faithful to the syntax and semantics of the original – I have even inserted line-references, so that those who wish can orientate the translation to an edition – but in some places I have been scandalously unfaithful. Sometimes this infidelity was a matter of mere tidiness. 'Bede's Death Song', for example. The original is five lines long (ten half-lines), and a terrifying wonder of compression and directness. Faithful to the compression, my translation originally came out at four-and-a-half lines (nine half-lines), so I inserted a half-line ('gleaned from its earning') which doesn't occur in the original, though I think Bede will probably forgive me. Then again there are half-lines – 'lǣne on londe' is a good example – whose literal translations I simply couldn't bring myself to commit to paper, so frequently had I seen them in student essays, exams, or other academic material. 'This dead life, transitory on land…'? I think not. My own version – note, *version* not 'translation' – is 'a deadened life of fidgets and flittings' ('The Seafarer'). I apologise to those who are spluttering over the texts of their long-unread student editions. Never mind, eh?

The diction of these translations will likewise be found unsatisfactory by those who have never read, and who do not intend to read, the originals. In truth I found 'diction' – word-choice, appropriacy – the most difficult aspect of translating, and that surprised me, given the severe challenges already posed by translating metrically and alliteratively. But it seems to me now that the poetic language of the originals included a highly stylised, genrespecific lexicon whose structure was at least partly arrived at because of the demands of alliteration. In this form of verse you simply do need one hell of a lot of synonyms for 'man', I'm afraid. The result is that the language of much Old English verse seems to bear the same relation to what I can reconstruct of the demotic as, say, the language of the Cranmer-inspired Prayer Book does to present-day English: it is probably a little bit above our heads. (I'm getting old enough to want to mumble 'And none the worse for that…') I tried, with no success I fear, to find the same relationship between poetic and demotic as existed in the originals. The alternative would have been to write non-alliteratively (which would have bored me in this context), or to offer paraphrases (which would in principle have been even more inaccurate), or to translate into prose (which would have been an impossibility – poems are poems).

*

Of the translations themselves I found working on the selections from *Beowulf* the most difficult. The difficulty interested me.

Stranded here in the twenty-first century it has become unfashionable to claim that any poem is inherently better than another. I have great sympathy with those whose entirely proper wish is to extend the canon of our readings in Old English, whose scepticism prompts them to look again at the metrics of, say, the Gnomic Verses as a corrective to the received unwisdoms of institutionalised 'Anglo-Saxon prosody' as this has been understood exclusively from the gifts of the *Beowulf* poet – or poets. There is much indeed that can still be learnt from what an earlier age acknowledged (if it was acknowledged at all) as the minor or the entirely peripheral. And yet, yes, *Beowulf* was a huge problem for me. I say that without wishing to clam explicitly that the difficulty was itself a measure of the greatness or even the particular merit of the original, but I suspect that it probably was – and is.

The difficulties were of different kinds.

Although it's the longest extant Old English poem, the original text is nevertheless hugely compressed. The poet (I shall continue to refer to him in the singular) makes ready use of metaphors, including those condensed compound metaphors called *kennings*. These are difficult for a translator to unpack without losing pace. One well-known example is the compound *gār-secg*, whose literal meaning is 'spear-man' but whose extended meaning, when used as a kenning, refers to the hostility of the open sea (e.g. *Beowulf*, 537b). How could I translate this? To risk writing 'we ventured out [as swimmers] onto the spear-man'? It sounded ridiculous. And so I found myself forced to paraphrase the kenning, while trying to keep its sense of temporal presence and animation: 'We... had once boasted... that we'd go, miles out, onto *the quickening sea*'. I had many a Polonian murmur over such lines: too weakly adjectival? What semantic work did the adjective actually do, within the translated poem? '"Quickening"... hmm? Yes, "quickening"'s quite good... Sense of both vitality and intensification... Hmm?'

The murmuring drove me mad, and lasted many months.

Another difficulty was syntactic. The *Beowulf* poet here and there makes ready use of grammatical structures which scholars sometimes have called 'interlaced': the sentence sets off happily, with an identifiable grammatical subject; one looks for a finite verb... and fails to find it until many half-lines later. In the interim, the verse twists into a digressive half-line, and then another; then there's another piece of structure, almost parenthetically giving a comment on some feature of the digression; then a further half-line comments on the parenthesis that has just commented on the digression that took place several half-lines back, until, finally, one reaches the finite verb that correlates with the original grammatical

11

subject, now feeling abandoned, lonely and half-forgotten, some-
where near the top of the same page.

The originating poet seemed to work half-line by half-line,
doling out information sometimes old, sometimes new, sometimes
immediately pertinent, sometimes apparently tangential. At its
best this technique is not only narrative, but revelatory, since the
reader (and listener) is confronted with the minor shocks of post-
posed information:

Cōm þā tō recede   rinc sīðian   (*Beowulf*, 720)

Fine: 'Then the travelling warrior [the reference is to Grendel, here
conceived simply, but ironically, as a *rinc*, a warrior] came to the
hall...' Yet the very next line gives postponed information: this *rinc*
is *drēamum bedǣled* 'deprived of joys' – an adjectival phrase whose
normative position in present-day English would immediately
precede the head noun, or immediately follow, and be appositional
to it. What to do? 'The deprived-of-dreams warrior'? Absolutely
not. 'This warrior, deprived of joys, came...' No. Time for a closer
look at the original case structure: *drēamum* is dative plural, there-
fore a translation in the genitive ('of joys') is suspect. Better
something like 'deprived with/from joys'... But that doesn't make
good sense in contemporary English. Better to capture the original
syntax by creating a compound adjective, *joy-deprived*, and
inserting that appositionally into the first half-line: 'So, joy-
deprived, the journeying man...' It was a fix of a sort, and the name
of the sort was – compromise. I havered among half-lines,
clutching at such compromise.

A final difficulty was of those many structural and thematic
digressions within the original. By 'digressions' I don't mean those
long pieces of almost cinematic re-telling familiar to all who have
studied *Beowulf*, nor those stories inserted into the main narrative
as more or less subtle illustrations of moral principle, or again, as
terrible warnings. I mean, rather, the way in which information is
refracted. Take Beowulf's fight with Grendel, for instance. The
reader comes to line 769, *Yrre wǣron begen* – both fighters were
enraged, furious – and expects lines 770ff. to introduce an explicit
narrative of what happened during the subsequent fight. (The poet
of 'Maldon' would have related exactly such an explicit narrative:
'X advanced – shook his ash-wood spear – intended injury – took
life from the marauding Viking – the marauding Viking lay on the
ground...') The *Beowulf* poet, though, is magnificently devious.
Much of the fight between Beowulf and Grendel is *refracted*, in the
sense that it is perceived *from the perspective of the structure of the hall*

in which the fight takes place: 'The frame of the hall resounded – miraculous that its rafters stood the combat, that it didn't fall apart, such a fair structure – but it had been strengthened inside and out by iron bands, skilful forge-work... Yet its furniture, including the many mead-benches, vibrated...' And so, just as Beowulf is tightening his terrible hammer-locks on Grendel's body, the reader and listener are directed to the effects of mutual fury on the furniture, with a further parenthetical comment on the nature of Heorot's fine reinforced masonry (or perhaps, its hinges).

Again I compromised, putting the furniture into graphically illustrative parentheses, and trying to keep the narrative line at least vaguely clear.

In the end I tried to be very glad indeed that I wasn't translating some of the great Norse poems, particularly the poems of the skalds, who 'were accustomed to interweave strands of sentences, giving first a part of one, then a part of the other, then reverting to the first' (Gordon, *An Introduction to Old Norse*, 1957: xli). Still, I'm glad I grappled with *Beowulf*, even though the murmuring was maddening. At times it felt as if the poet had dashed the mirror of his understanding onto the nearest rock, so refracted was the story... It glittered from shards, was lit in fragments. And yet, at best, it was that same poet's sheer technique that allows his reader or listener the chances to apprehend the different aspects of the story so simultaneously and multi-dimensionally: the physical and the moral, time past and time present, were caught and held there, in the same glistering, strange yet inevitable half-lines.

*

In some cases I used those editions of the poems that lie on the bookshelves of my library, in others (principally some of the riddles) I used versions of original texts as these are found in handbooks, textbooks and anthologies. I was hugely grateful for the editions and their glossaries. At all times I had access to the *Dictionary of Old English*, as well as to the second edition of the OED. I worked throughout in pencil, in a large workbook, later transferring the handwritten texts into electronic files. It interests me somewhat that I work in the same way with my own poems. It is only with prose written directly or indirectly for money that I can apparently work straight into the computer.

In certain places I have accepted without comment some emendations that have been proposed, usually on ill-understood metrical grounds, by earlier editors. To comment fully on these emendations, and to justify every choice, would have been to fill each page with footnotes. However, I can say with unusual justice that when I made choices between, say, manuscript readings, or accepted emendations, I always chose in such a way as to make a kind of poetic sense – that is, sense as this is consistent with the revealed world of the poem. A good example of this is the first line of 'Deor', which opens *Wēlund him be wurman wræces cunnade*. As Richard Hamer notes in his splendid little volume of translations, '*be wurman* has defied explanation'. By serpents? Dragons? By the tribe known as the Vermar? On the other hand, though it is in scholarly terms unsatisfying, the reading *be wymman* ('by women') makes poetic sense as well as being at least possible palaeographically, and thematically, consistent with the mythical life of Weland. And so it is this reading I have preferred.

Elsewhere, and once again in terms of diction, I have used many compound words. These are metrically most important, not least in those half-lines Sievers dubbed D and E. But however useful they might be metrically, some of the compounds I have used will never be found in the OED. An example is 'one-treader', which I use to translate *eardstapa* (literally, 'earth-stepper') in 'The Wanderer'. Behind my chosen compound lies, of course, the word 'al-one', whose imaginative world is that of agonisingly solitary footsteps making a journey into poetic sense.

*

It is well to remember that the poems, with the exception of those written and signed by Cynewulf (which for reasons of space are not represented here), are anonymous. In the manuscripts they are written out margin-to-margin – vellum was relatively costly, and therefore space could not be wasted. No poem is given a title in manuscript. It irks me now and then that poems are sometimes glibly referred to as (for example) 'The Seafarer', or 'The Battle of Maldon'. I start to twitch, since such a careless, though customary, ascription of titles itself sets up generic expectations which are not fulfilled – and never could be fulfilled – by the imaginative world limned in the poems. Worst in this respect is the poem known as 'The Wanderer'. 'Wanderer' always makes me think of Schubert or Liszt – but they depict a world of Romantic melancholy very far removed from that of the protagonist of the Old English poem, and it is muddle-headed to allow any feeling of Romantic melancholy to pervade our encounter with the mysterious, rigorous agony explored there.

Still, the poems have been given their titles, and there's no point railing at nomenclature which has been hallowed by use. Further, I don't expect any publisher would have found it attractive or useful to publish translations whose titles were for instance 'folios 45–7 of

14

the Exeter Book'. Therefore I have stuck, grumbling silently, with the time-stained titles.

Complete texts are included of all works except *Beowulf*, of which I have translated only substantial fragments. In some poems, however, it has proved impossible to translate complete texts, for the simple reason that the manuscript is either radically corrupt or damaged. In other places, too, some few half-lines appear to be missing; these last are cases probably attributable to scribal error. Generally, where material is missing from the original manuscript I have not attempted to supply material of my own, but have instead used dots to mark the missing material (e.g. at the beginning of 'The Battle of Maldon', in 'The Ruin' and elsewhere). I'm afraid a full and informed discussion of missing material, manuscript damage and scribal error would have required me to construct new scholarly editions of the works concerned, rather than poetic translations, and therefore the reader must endure the very occasional clumsiness and shorthand of a row of dots.

*

Variety, attractiveness, then, aligned with metrical plausibility. These were the desiderata out of which I was writing. I also dared to hope that this small selection of translations would be useful enough, particularly to those coming at these poems for the first time, to want to make readers go back to the originals and their editions, and begin for themselves those encounters which have sustained me for half a lifetime and which have meant that occasionally I look up and shake my head in bewilderment, not so much because everything changed, but because it all, and in so many profound senses, has remained the same.

Acknowledgements

Many people contributed to the making of these translations. My most direct and immediate intellectual debt is to Steve Glosecki, formerly of the University of Alabama at Birmingham, whose death in 2007 left the world without a huge-hearted, generous, wise and humane presence. Still, when it appears, Steve's translation of *Beowulf* will take its place alongside the greatest of the great Old English translations, and from that work, as well as from our enduring friendship and correspondence, I learned more than I can duly acknowledge in this note.

To other friends and former colleagues – to Grevel Lindop,

Helen Maclean, Rob Rollison, Copland Smith, and many others – I offer my warmest thanks. These people either were prepared to discuss the most puzzling aspects of translation, or they were good enough to read and comment on draft material. The encouragement helped enormously, because it challenged me into as much clarity as I could express in the new poems. I am also, and particularly, grateful to Marjoke Kuipers, who read through, and questioned, successive drafts of what I had done, and did so in ways that provoked me into further clarity, economy, and common sense. *Dank je wel*.

Here I would also like to thank Bruce Hayes, whose graduate seminars I attended (far too sporadically) at UCLA in 1995. His ground-breaking researches into the number and nature of metrical constraints provided me with a starting-point from which I developed some of the principles underlying these translations, though I was too dim to realise it at the time.

To older faces and voices – particularly to those who taught me Old English at the University of Newcastle-upon-Tyne (1979–82) – I wish to say that time has confirmed what an uncertain intelligence suspected all those years ago. Your teaching has helped to sustain me for thirty years, and somehow enlarged my comprehension so that it could love these poems, even when it did not fully understand them. That was a great gift, and I thank you for it.

'The Seafarer' appeared in a 2007 issue of *PN Review*. To Michael Schmidt I offer warmest thanks for allowing me to use the translation unchanged in the present context. To Michael, too, and to Carcanet, who helped me not only to develop whatever poetic voices I have but also allowed me to use them, I am, as always, most deeply grateful.

Chris McCully

References and Further Reading

Bliss, A.J. 1958. *The Metre of* Beowulf. Oxford: Blackwell.

—— 1962. *An Introduction to Old English Metre*. Oxford: Blackwell.

Cable, Thomas. 1991. *The English Alliterative Tradition*. Philadelphia: University of Pennsylvania Press.

Creed, R.P. 1966. 'A new approach to the rhythm of *Beowulf*'. *PMLA* 81: 23–33.

Dunning, T.P. and A.J. Bliss, eds. 1969. *The Wanderer*. London: Methuen.

Fulk, R.D. 1992. *A History of Old English Meter*. Philadelphia: University of Pennsylvania Press.

Getty, Michael. 2002. *The Metre of* Beowulf: *A Constraint-based Approach*. Berlin and New York: Mouton de Gruyter.

Gordon, E.V. 1957. *An Introduction to Old Norse*. 2nd edition. Oxford: Clarendon Press.

Gordon, I. ed. 1979. *The Seafarer*. Manchester: Manchester University Press.

Hamer, Richard. 1970. *A Choice of Anglo-Saxon Verse*. London: Faber and Faber.

Hayes, Bruce. 1995. *Metrical Stress Theory: principles and case studies*. London: University of Chicago Press.

Heusler, A. 1929. 'Deutsche Versgeschichte, mit Einschluss des Altenglischen und Altnordischen Stabreimverses'. In Hermann Paul, ed., 1925–9, *Grundriss der Germanischen Philologie*. Vol. III. Berlin and Leipzig: Walter de Gruyter and Co.

Klaeber, F. 1950. *Beowulf, and the Fight at Finnsburg*. 3rd edition. Lexington, Mass.: D.C. Heath.

Leslie, R.F. ed. 1961. *Three Old English Elegies*. Manchester: Manchester University Press.

McCully, C.B. and J.J. Anderson, eds. 1996. *English Historical Metrics*. Cambridge: Cambridge University Press.

McCully, Chris and Sharon Hilles. 2005. *The Earliest English*. London and New York: Pearson Education. [Chapter 5 is a relatively formal, though still basic, introduction to Old English metrics.]

Mitchell, Bruce and Fred C. Robinson. 1992. *A Guide to Old English*. 5th edition. Oxford: Blackwell.

Obst, Wolfgang. 1987. *Der Rhythmus des* Beowulf. Heidelberg: Carl Winter Universitätsverlag.

Pope. J.C. 1942. *The Rhythm of* Beowulf. New Haven: Yale University Press. [2nd edition, 1966, contains some revisions.]

Quirk, Randolph, V. Adams and D. Davy. 1975. *Old English Literature: A Practical Introduction*. London: Edward Arnold.

Russom, G. 1987. *Old English Meter and Linguistic Theory*. Cambridge: Cambridge University Press.

Shippey, T.A. 1972. *Old English Verse*. London: Hutchinson.

Sievers, E. 1885. 'Zur Rhythmik des Germanischen Alliterationsverses.' *Beiträge zur Geschichte der Deutsche Sprache und Literatur* 10: 209–314; 451–545

Swanton, Michael, ed. 1970. *The Dream of the Rood*. Manchester: Manchester University Press.

Tolkien, J.R.R. 1936. '*Beowulf*: the monsters and the critics'. *Proceedings of the British Academy* XXII. Oxford: Oxford University Press.

Wrenn, C.L. 1973. *Beowulf, with the Finnesburg Fragment*. 3rd edition, revised by W.F. Bolton. London: Harrap.

A Note on Manuscripts, Libraries and the Internet

A very good, non-technical and wonderfully illustrated introduction to Anglo-Saxon manuscripts is Michelle P. Brown, *Anglo-Saxon Manuscripts* (London: The British Library, 1991).

Four great codices contain between them over two-thirds of the Old English verse still known to us. They are the Vercelli Book (Cathedral Library, Vercelli), which contains 'The Dream of the Rood' as well as two poems signed in runes by Cynewulf; the Exeter Book (Exeter Cathedral Library, MS 3501), which contains all the elegies and the vast majority of the riddles; the Junius Manuscript (Bodleian MS. Junius 11), which contains the poems 'Genesis', 'Exodus', 'Daniel' and 'Christ and Satan'; and the Beowulf Manuscript (British Library Cotton Vitellius A.XV), which contains 'Judith' as well as 'Beowulf'.

Facsimile versions of these codices are available in some university libraries. Among them (and works I have myself consulted) are *The Exeter Book of Old English Poetry*, ed. R.W. Chambers, M. Förster and R. Flower (London, 1933) and *Beowulf*, ed. J. Zupitza, 2nd edition (with notes by Norman Davis, Early English Text Society, 1959).

For those with little or no access to university libraries holding the original manuscripts or their facsimiles, something can still be achieved by browsing the Internet. (Such browsing can incidentally give the browser some idea of the vitality and beauty of Anglo-Saxon manuscript art and decoration.) Michelle Brown (see above) offers a short course on Anglo-Saxon manuscripts at www.fathom.com/course/10701049/Index.html. These pages include some images. Anglo-Saxon Manuscripts in Microfiche Facsimile (ASMMF) is a project which makes Anglo-Saxon manuscripts available electronically. Manuscripts are available by subscription or by individual volume (www.mendota.english. wisc.edu/~ASMMF/index.htm). The small collection of Anglo-Saxon manuscripts held by Trinity College, Cambridge, has a website which includes some lovely illustrations. See for example the richly decorated title page to the opening of John's Gospel (www.trin.cam.ac.uk/sdk13/asmss.html). A specimen page from the Exeter Book may be viewed at www.exeter-cathedral. org.uk/Gallery/Library/L01.html.

The assiduous browser will uncover many such useful sites. Search terms might include *anglo saxon manuscripts*; *exeter book*;

vercelli book; beowulf manuscript; junius manuscript; anglo saxon manuscript facsimile; british library. Some magnificent manuscript illustrations can be found be using search terms such as *lindisfarne gospels; book of kells.* Other sites offer Old English versions of the texts, and/or translations. These can be just as idiosyncratic as my own work, and therefore such versions should ideally be used alongside a reputable scholarly edition of the same text (or manuscript facsimile).

The Wanderer

for Henk Aertsen

'Wanderer, one-treader:
mind-torn in mercy
struggles ocean streams –
stirs ice-locked seas
and wretched his spoor,
So spoke the earth-stepper,
cleft brood of killing,
'Often each daybreak
to count my cares.
with whom I could talk,
my thrall of thoughts.
this is the craft, custom:
what treasured in mind,
Whatsoever a man thinks
nor can his worn-out zeal
nor his hurt heart-mood
Each traveller through time,
must be silent about sorrow
I, thus, exiled,
and far from friends,
and mind's lament,
I dealt darkness
and graved him in ground
From there I went wretched,
crossed ocean's ice
new patrons, new powers –
of home or of hall,
befriend their friendless
wean care from worry.
when it keeps in step
of one who has no one
is twinned by the outlaw,
knows the spirit's ice,
Bond-friends he recalls,
gold-gifts of youth
by his peerless prince…
That counsel, that care

care-worn often,
of Measurer's grace,
long the estranging –
with aching hands,
forceful fate's wrath.'   5
agony in mind's-eye:
kinfolk fallen.
my due was, stricken,
Of the quick, none are left
or tell openly   10
In thanes' company
what's caught in memory,
is kept tacit.
is a thankless gift,
resist his doom   15
heal him or help him.
tasked with sadness,
on the self's journey.
on alien earth
have fettered both mouth   20
since many years ago
to my doom-lord
where no gold-joy was.
racked by winter,
in order to seek   25
the undeprived
who would hear my words,
face over feasting,
Cruel, grief is cruel
with the stricken traverse   30
needing or missing them,
not the twisted gold;
not the earth's glory.
and the boon-giving –
granted in feasting   35
Perished all those days!
can't now return.

Long that parting,
But when sorrow and sleep
to rack the wretched,
then, then he imagines
the neck-clasp and kissing,
of head and hands –
when his lord lavished him
Then, fetched from sleep,
wakes to the prospect
solitary sea-birds,
rime-frost; snow-storm
Hard, those woundings;
longing for the lost one;
Still memory meets
gratefully regards
those its companions.
those fleeting spirits
no familiar cries.
to the one forced to travel
worn out wave-paths,
Understand rightly:
why my scant deeming
if I think deeply
how they of an instant
quick once, then quelled –
each day and every day
It cannot be managed,
of the passing winters.
not too hot-hearted,
nor too weak a warrior,
nor too tender, nor too timid;
or boasting's repute…
await prayer,
underpin all pride,
know where it must turn,
Terrible, it will be terrible
when all riches of the world
just as now, today,
old walls stand awry
buildings are snow-swept,
Vanished are the wine-halls;
lie deprived of prayer.
mounds of corpses.
fared them further:

that lost friendship.
dissemble together
unreasoning one,   40
his thane's embrace,
kneeling to pay homage
how, once, it was,
long worlds ago.
the friendless one   45
of winter, of waves;
a swath of feathers;
rife with hail-stone.
heart is heavier
and losses come again.   50
mind's every part,
and eagerly greets
But they drift away:
fetch no comfort,
Cares come again   55
the terrors of himself:
wastes of ocean…
no reason in the world
should not become darkened
over the doom of men,   60
ailed, were abandoned –
just as this crust of earth
falls to idleness; fails.
but requires wisdom
Patience must, friend: 65
nor hasty of speech;
nor too wilful;
nor too tempted by gain
Pay rite of passage,
so that their promises shall   70
and the preening thought
tend all its troubles.
for the true-sighted
are wrecked by time –
on the doomed world's crust   75
and are wind-stricken,
snecked by ice-candles.
vanquisher, victim
Pride? Extinguished:
Combat took some,   80
this one the storm-fowl carried

over ocean's deep;
by grinning hoar-wolf;
graved his gold-friend
The Shaper destroys,
and correct judgement
old works of giants
Whosoever, instinct,
who has fathomed furthest
often must remember
from a wise distance
What has become of the horse? Of the hand?

What has become of the feasting-places?

O unshattered cup!
O prince's power!
struck numb under night –
Vestiges, relics
the lost faces
the hurled ash-shafts
feed on them – carrion.
And storms batter
snow-showers sweep them,
the ravening sky –
unquelled darkness –
sends hail, nail-storms,
All struggles, all is spent
world turns, fractious;
Property vanishes;
mankind vanishes;
All made in time
So he spoke, runing
Yet may good fall to one

who renders remedy

whose conduct is courage.

a hope of heaven

to this one death was dealt
and this one… Gallow-faced he
in the gaunt earth's depth.
shatters the habitudes,   85
brings no rejoicing:
stand everywhere idle.
inward and canny,
down fate's darkness,
age-old slaughter,   90
deal out these words:
What has become of the hoard-sharer?
Of the fair dwellings?
O the shining mail-coat!
Perished in time-dark,   95
as if they never had been!
are vested, in place:
stand under the fire-blackened wall,
hand death to them,
Their fate is ordained.   100
stone-slopes of earth,
shackle them in winter;
ripped by nightfall,
from squalling North
hardship for men.   105
on the span of earth:
fate-stroke is fickle.
patron vanishes;
kindred… All vanish.
was mortal, useless.'   110
at wisdom's rim.
who guards his faith rightly,
whose grief remains silent;
for bitterness of mind,
for the wreckage of hope;
Care-worn, mind-torn,
may his grace be mercy,
that offers to all
a home, haven.   115

A Riddle

from the Exeter Book

My dress? Darkness,
though each adornment's bright,
red-glittering, sheer:
shining costume.
I misdirect
the reckless, guide a fool
on his fool's errand.
Others I stay from
necessary journeys.
No way of knowing   5
why they, maddened,
all thought stolen,
all acts aimless,
should amplify me –
waste, wrong-doing!
And they'll have woe for it
once Consequence comes,
unclasps its care-hoard,
if they haven't yet stopped,
are still obsessed.   10

Deor

Women did for Wayland.
the obsessed smith-god
for travel companion
winter's exile;
after Nithhad's supple
brutally, had condemned
May this, may this

Inward with woe
suffered sorrow's all:
torment and longing,
wretchedness was fated
sinew-brace had bound,　　　5
the better of men.
as that pass away.

The death of brothers?
was less grievous sore,
over-obvious,
she'd become pregnant.
simply decided
May this, may this

To Beadohild it meant less,
than her own self's trouble:
easy to discover　　　10
In panic, she couldn't think,
to settle for the worst.
as that pass away?

We heard many could tell
dreaming of water,
was sleep-deprived.
May this, may this

of Meathhild's plight –
the wife of Geat　　　15
Sorrow made her love.
as that pass away.

And Theodric?
too many knew how
May this, may this

For thirty years
he ruled Mearingburgh.
as that pass away?　　　20

We entered the mind
a world of wolves.
spanned Gothic peoples:
Many of the finest
expected only pain,
that such a kingdom
May this, may this

of Ermanric's thought:
His wide empire
grim sovereignty.
lived fettered by sorrows,
and prayed always　　　25
might be overcome.
as that pass away.

Sorrow-care abides,
dark-steeped in mind.
that his dole of doom's
And yet imagine:
it's a witting God

blanked of blessings,
To a man's self it seems
durable, endless.　　　30
among the world
grants change on change,

assurance to some,
while to some, others,
And now something
Once their harp-voice,
I was loved by my lord –
Many were the winters
praised by patrons,
astute singer –
lords once lavished on,
May this, may this

to some graceful,
he assigns sorrows.
of myself, my Self: 35
the Heodenings' song-maker,
dear loved, dear named.
I waxed in my song,
until Heorrenda – proud,
stole that estate   40
once left to me.
as that pass away?

A Riddle

from the Exeter Book

My home's noisy.   I'm not. I'm mute
in this dwelling-place.   A deity shaped
our twinned journey.   I'm more turbulent than he,
at times stronger.   He's tougher – durable.
Sometimes I come to rest. He always runs on ahead.   5
For as long as I shall live I shall live in him.
If we undo ourselves,   death's due claims me.

Caedmon's Hymn

for Richard Bailey

Now we must praise him,
the Measurer's might,
works wondrous-fathered –
eternal Strength,
In the beginning he shaped
a heaven as a roof,
Then middle-earth:
the eternal Strength,
the land below.

heaven-span's high Prince;
mind, and conception;
since of all wonders He,
established the source.
for those begotten of men   5
holy Maker.
Monarch spanning men,
in time furnished
Lord, everlasting!

A Riddle

from the Exeter Book

A man walked in.
careful in counsel,
He had only one eye,
and was two-footed,
Hunch-backed he was…
with shoulders, arms,
atop his two sides.

Many sat runing,
whose courage was wise.
but ears… Yes, two,
but with twelve-hundred heads.
…with two hands, a belly,   5
and with one long neck
Say what he's called.

The Seafarer

for Derek Britton

Truth? I can seal it
tell its stories:
I owned often,
how I've borne both
known sorrow's surges
wave-roiling terror –
the narrow night-watch
as the cliffs unsteadied.
my feet fettered,
clamped, ice-locked, though
hot round the heart,
at the spirit's tiredness.
those day-dawdlers
how I lived winter,
on the exile's path,
deprived alike
frost-candles in clothes,
Nothing to hear there
on terror's frozen track.
were diversion, a game,
whaup's weeping-song
gulls' aimless cry
Tempests beat stone-cliffs,
ice-feathered one;
screamed, dew-feathered.
befriended my desolate
Hard to believe it
suburb-dwelling saps
for the wine-flushed, sottish,
having to last, to wait
Night-shower nipped,
rime-frost on earth-crust;
each grain coldest.
terror of imagining:
must I myself travel,
Yet I must, I must.
to this due journey.

in song's reckoning,
times of hardship
unease and toil;
bitterness and breast-care,
in the surging keel,   5
they wore me, saw
nailed to the boat-prow
Cold, constriction:
frost-bound and cramped,
my cares ravened there,   10
and hunger tore
Time's slaves can't imagine –
dwelling fair on land –
wretched, sorrowful,
an ice-cold sea,   15
of praise, friends, profit,
flogged by hail-nails…
but the hail, sea-yell
At times, swan-voices
or gannet's pluming –   20
instead of the world's laughter;
instead of the good mead-drink.
and the tern answered,
often eagle-kites
And yet scant or none   25
winter-faring.
for land-lubbers,
with no sense alert,
but I was weary there,
on the lanes of sea.   30
and from the North, snow-squall;
rife hail-stones' pelt,
And a cauldron of thought,
Onto such towering seas
onto the torn wave's holm?   35
Moments compel me
My duty's to seek

land out of longing,
But there's no man on earth –
not with goodness, nor gifts;
nor so lavish in deed
who isn't anxious
what god guide him,
Harp-song's irrelevant,
the pleasuring of women,
nothing matters more than
dangerous longing
Trees shake with blossom,
and meadows brighten,
but the quickening warns
drives the heart-thought
and onto the tide-races,
Still the cuckoo calls,
summer's guardian sings,
bitterness, resentful.
nestled in his nothings,
of such vicious voyages,
Promise, compulsion
and mine is mettled
ranges the whale-way,
the ocean's sheets –
greedy, more eager
still yells of death
urges me onward;
dearer and more dreadful
of fidgets and flittings.
that nothing shall last
of the world. And one
will always throw doubt
old age; sickness;
each can bring judgement
'Reputation,' then?
tell afterwards
who must earn opinion
contending in time
opposing the devil
so that children to come
and their name number
always, always,
know bliss with the blessed.

land more lasting…
not with courage for manners;
nor so gracious in youth;   40
or so loved by kings –
about what the ocean might claim,
go where he will.
as is ring-giving,
the promises of the world –   45
noise of the sea-roll,
for doomed voyages.
the towns grow fair
the world quickens –
worry to its journey   50
from its dithering
tracks of the ocean.
its cadence lament:
then sorrow's ordained,
Blessed is the citizen,   55
who knows nothing
nor ventures their limits.
can't imprison a mind,
by the mere's slow flood,
the whole world's expanse,   60
and always returns
for going. Though the cuckoo
an irresistible Yes
aches, God-given,
than a deadened life   65
It's failure that warns
of the noise and wealth
of these witnessing three
in the eyes of hours:
or the sword's envy –   70
at any just moment.
The ruck of the living
of the talents of men,
before they end their span,
with the tall hatreds,   75
with purity of deed,
will have chance to praise
among the new angels
so that honour will last,
                                                             80

Now blanked are the days,

all the opulence of earth's kingdom:
no real rulers; no royalty left,
nor gold-giving granted as once there was.
Our ancestors shared honour between them,
enjoyed justice, were juried by fame… 85
But crumbled, declined is that cache of dreams.
Now the world's witnessed only by the weaker ones,
possessed by the hiss of sin. Hand-shake's despised,
decency withers, and decadence is rife
in the human souls inhabiting the earth. 90
Age shall wither them in turn. Ashen,
they'll mourn, grey-haired, the merits of the past –
greatness, generosity given back to time.
And when the flesh-home, the body,
                                  starts to fail the spirit
they won't taste sweetness but traffic in sorrow, 95
and – motionless – imagine the might-have-been.
Brother buries brother, buries gold in graves.
Clan and kinsman are corpses, whose shrouds
sag with blood-money, booty of conscience.
But to the soul that's sick, whose sin chokes it, 100
money brings no merit, no mercy from God,
however it's hoarded in the here and now.
Great is God's power, that girds even
                                  the foundations of earth,
establishing forever the strong earth's crust,
the land's fineness, the firmament's roof. 105
Who won't dread his Redeemer
                                  will die a fool – unprepared
                                  for death's swiftness,
but who lives humbly shall have his reward
                                  from heaven's benison.
The Measurer's strength shall install fortitude,
                                  presence in the powerless.
Yet a man's self-control must be trained, his mind
                                  made steadfast, resolute.
He should honour promises, purity of manner. 110
It is moderation that's the most of man –
faced with friend or foe, a refined conscience.
Though foe will be fire, conflagration,
so also the friend whose fate's unwished.
But nevertheless God's knowing is great, 115
his justice more just, more genuine
                                  than any man's deeming.

Where, after all, is our home?
We should give our thanks,
and our long labour,
to its appointed place,
whose life is vivid
in heavenly hope.
The Elder of Days
Eternal Strength

Our homecoming?
thoughts to the journey,
so that longing shall pass
praise the blessedness   120
in the love of God,
To the Holy Lord, praise!
honoured and raised us,
stretched through eternity.
Amen.

A Riddle

from the Exeter Book

for Copland Smith

If I stay at home;
if I tread through mud –
And yet sometimes
by my trappings,
driven by cloud-strength,
over nations, dwelling-places.
sings from my war-shirt;
glitters, pinioned,
flood-plain nor furrow,

if I stir water;
mute, my song's-raiment.
I'm swept aloft
turn over rooftops
borne into distance   5
And now melody
wind-song's lexicon
when I grace neither
but am firmament's guest.

The Dream of the Rood

in memory of Barbara Strang

To tell, to limb
what I met with –
when saying is asleep?
It seemed I saw
was raised into space,
most intense brilliants:
dew-drenched with gold.
embedded in earth's-eye:
glittered on this gallows,

comprehended and adored.

spirits blessed through aeons;
this long Creation –
Stunning, strife's loveliness –
I was stained, injured,
glimmered in its garments,
dripping gold-filigree.
that effortlessly clothed
Yet caught in the gold
envy of ages,
whose tear leaked down

afraid, fearing

changed hue, harness:
soiled by sweat's-flow;

Still I stayed watching
sorrowful – seeing
witnessing miracle,
chose wood also to witness.
It was years ago –
Hard from holt's-edge
stripped from standpoint.
for the many made me

the loveliest of dreams,
midnight's moment
Surely. Listen.
sumptuousness. A tree
wrapped round with light,   5
a beacon, completely
Gem-stones studded it,
beautiful, that five such
whose gaze angels –
first fair of time –
But what hung there was no
    crime: 10
spoilt humankind;
all looked on, rapt.
but stricken, sinning, I:
apprehending how this tree
glistered wonderfully,   15
Diamond was light
this forest's emblem.
I could discern
an arrow-tear
the limb's right side.   20
And I was lost in sorrow,
how fair this vision,
whose central symbol
now heavy with blood,
and now set with light,
hoarded sweetness.
this stem of time,
the Saviour's tree,   25
until at once it spoke,
Its words were these:
yet I remember.
I was hewn, stricken,
Stronger ones seized me,   30
a spectacle, mockery,
spite for malefactors.

35

They bore me away on their shoulders, set me
on a hill, fastened
evil-doers onto me. Then I saw the Elder of mankind
hasten there, purposed, hurry to embrace me.
And against the Dear One's word would I dare ever   35
to bend down or break, though I saw the baleful
and blent earth tremble? All adversaries
I could have felled there – but firm I stood.
The young hero ungirded. He
was God: all-purposed,
strong, and endless. Onto that stern gallows   40
He climbed, whose courage
was seen by many; whose meaning there
was mankind's release.
I shook, shuddered at His embrace, but shatter
or stoop to earth's-fold
I didn't dare, nor fall: still fast I stood.
I was the rood, reared up. I raised the Omnipotent,
Dear Prince of heaven – nor dared to bend.   45
Blood-darkened nails they nailed through me,
death-wounds, still visible,
open wounds of malice. Injury I did none,
not one, nor dared any.
The two of us they smeared, tortured together,
all of me blood-drenched
from the ripped side of Man, who hung there
reft, after spirit's surrender.
Many were the destinies whose meaning I endured.   50
Hostile was the hill whose Lord of hosts
was nailed, racked there. And nightfall covered
the quelled radiance, the corpse of God,
with cloud. And shadow shook from shadow
under an ailing heaven. All Creation wept,   55
grieving a king's-death whose cross was Christ.
Two came walking from the wan
    distance
towards the warrior – I was aware of it all –
and I was stricken, shot through with sorrow, now bending
to men's hands
willingly, humbly. And there they held all-wielding
God,   60
lifted Him from limitless torment. And then they left me,
those battle-retainers,
standing girdled in moisture, completely maimed

by arrow's-graze.
They laid down the limb-weary, *stood at the head*
of His lovely body,

beheld heaven's Lord *while He rested,*
a moment's exhaustion

after victory's winning. *A vault for Him* 65
they began to make,

those men, in the sight *of His slayer.*
From bright stone they carved it,

setting within it *the Sealer of triumph,*
and singing sorrow-songs

as evening ailed – *and ailing, departed,*
drained, from the Dear One. *His due was to rest,*
reft of company.

Grieving, still lamenting, *for a good while we* 70
stood in position *while stricken voices*
of war-bands went up. *His body began to cool,*
bright house of life. *And at last... We were hewn,*
felled, razed to earth – *of all earthly fates*
the most dreadful!

They buried us deep *in a pit. In time's pattern* 75
the Lord's people,

friends, found us there...
and I was girded *with gold, silver.*
 And now you have listened, *beloved Christ-soldier,*
to how I endured it – *destiny's evil,*
most sore of sorrows. *But now on the sill of time* 80
men, multitudes, *muster of Creation,*
shall honour, praise me *henceforth and everywhere,*
prayerfully choose me. *On me the Child of God*
suffered, endured once; *drenched with glory*
my height spans to heaven, *and healing is my gift* 85
to each, everyone *whose awe comprehends me.*
Once long ago *I was the worst torment,*
most loathed on earth, *until the life-way*
I could open to all *users of witness.*
Thus the Elder of Days *deemed me, honoured me* 90
above all holt-wood, *heaven's Guardian,*
just as His mother, Mary, *was manifold, blessed*
by Almighty God *for men on earth,*
was venerated *above all woman-kind.*
 I command you now, *my marcher in Christ,* 95
to reveal this vision, *give it voice among men,*
limb in language *this Lustre-tree*

that Almighty God
for the multiple sins
and for Adam's
Death He tasted –
in plenitude, in power,
then ascended to heaven.
on middle-earth
on the day of doom
Almighty God
whose aim shall be to judge –
each, everyone
they have earned for themselves
None – no, not any –
of those very words
In front of multitudes
where that one might be
would taste death's bitterness
But they'll be afraid, and few,
what they might begin to say
Yet none – not any –
who carry in their breasts
And by means of that Rood
will construct its heaven
each who intends an

      Prayer I directed,
that had inspired wonder.
completely alone,
for its journey forth,
with the kind of hope
May I now seek out
alone, and more often
and worship it well.
fills all my spirit,
lies in prayer to the Cross.
I have none left on earth:
world's faithlessness

living now in heaven
joy beyond judgement.
and wait daily
the Cross of the Lord,
revealed on earth,
me from the moments
and bring me to the bliss

grappled with, endured on
mankind committed
oldest of wrongs.   100
yet in doom arose
whose purpose was Man;
Here once again
Man will be sought for
by the Deemer himself,   105
gathered among angels,
Endless Juror –
for what honour (or none)
in this short ambit.
shall be unafraid   110
the Wielder shall speak.
the Almighty shall ask
who, mastered by Christ,
as He did, once, on the sill of time.
and will fail to know   115
when God tasks them.
need be afraid
the beauty of the Cross.
each mortal soul
from the stress of time –   120
eternal dwelling-place.
rapt, to the symbol
My spirit was alone –
but with longing anew
suffused altogether   125
that is hope's zenith.
need's victory over sorrow
than all other men,
My want of that
and my faith's patron   130
Of powerful friends
all have departed
and find themselves
where they find Glory's King,
with the Lord of Hosts,
That justice I expect,   135
for that dear time when
that I encountered once
shall eventually fetch
of this mortal life
of bountiful heaven   140

where the Lord's servants
at the endless feast,
Time He will set me,
where I shall take my place
reverence His glory.
He who endured
the gallows-tree,
and a home in heaven,
when he dared Hell's fire.
dear Son triumphant
whose might returned
a host of souls,
to the Almighty One,
and all the saints
gathered in glory
Creator of Power,

are lavished, seated
always. There through all
an eternal Ever
and praise Him where His saints
May God be my friend –   145
for humankind
gave back our life
our hope renewed
Durance was blessed,
on that expedition,   150
with a multitude,
to heaven's kingdom,
whose angels, new-made,
who had always been,
as their God came home,
to the peace of His country.

Bede's Death Song

None shall become –
so knowing, so wise,
before that hence-going
after its dying day
gleaned from his earning

faced with his need-journey –
that he should not reconsider
how his spirit
will be dealt judgement
of evil or of good.   5

The Fight at Finnsburg

…shall torch gables.'
Hnaef then replied,
prince young in war:
'That is no day dawning.
No dragon flies here,
nor are hall's gables
aglow with fire.
It's battle stalks us.
Its birds gather; 5
the grey wolf's yelling;
every weapon resounds,
shield answers shaft.
Now shines the moon,
wandering the heavens.
Now woe's woken,
forcing affliction
on these fated kin.
Now also wake,
warriors of mine! 10
Grip shields tightly,
turn thoughts to valour
and the brave vanguard.
Be resolute now!'
Many a gold-decorated
guard stood up then,
each gripping his sword.

Sigferth and Eaha,
their swords unsheathed,
went to one doorway –
doughty defenders – 15
while at the other doorway
stood Ordlaf and Guthlaf,
Hengest himself
hard on their footprints.
Still Guthere
urged Garulf – that Spear –
not to risk his life
bravely in the rush,
hard crush of battle
around the hall's doorway, 20
when untamed hatred
would take it away.
And he asked loudly,
unhesitating
and great-hearted,
who guarded the doors.
'Sigeferth's my name,
of the Secgan clan,'
he said, 'a famed fighter.
I've seen my fill of woes, 25
of strife's struggle.
Whether *you* will be stricken
Fate's deemed already.
Your doom lies with me.'
In that desperate place
din of carnage,
cruel hands at work,
curved shields shattering,
hard helmets, bodies…
The boards thundered. 30
Garulf was first
to fall. Combat
deprived its hosts,
those perishable ones,
of Guthlaf's son,
and a good many with him
became corpses.
Now the carrion-raven
circled, sallow-feathered.
Sword-light flickered 35
as if all Finnsburg
were flame-riddled.
I've never yet heard tell
of truer warriors
than those sixty souls
so courageously

endowed, nor of the merit   of dewy mead
so deserving, than those men   whose mettle was Hnaef's.   40
Five days they fought: five days. None fell.
Those fierce kinsmen   kept defending the doors.
One warrior then   went on his way –
his corselet sheared,   he said, armour
shattered, helmet-front   holed by the encounter.   45
His captain at once   enquired of the man
how bravely his kin   were bearing their wounds,
whether any of the young…

A Charm

Against bee-swarm
Take earth. Throw it with your right hand under your right foot,
saying:

You've been fetched underfoot,   can now be found there.
So earth avails   against all and everything –
and against malice,   and against ingratitude,
and against the manifold tongues of mockers, gainsayers.

And afterwards throw earth whenever they swarm, saying:

Sit down, strife-woman!   Sink back to earth.
You never wanted   to fly off to the wood.
You're as mindful, covetous   of things that are mine
as fond Everyman   of food and lodging!

Wulf and Eadwacer

It's as though a kind of gift   had been given to my people.
If he comes vicious   it's him they'll want to capture.
We're differently placed.
On that island, Wulf;   I on this other.
Secure, that isle   caught among fenland.   5
Murder-minded,   men who inhabit it.
If he comes vicious   it's him they'll want to capture.
We are apart.
Over that wide distance   it's for Wulf I've longed.
Then it was rainy weather,   *and I rigid, weeping*   10
when his battledress   *began to embrace me…*
I took pleasure in it;   it was pain also.
Wulf – O my Wulf!   What wastes me now
is your absence,   infrequent visits,
lacklustre spirit,   not the lack of food.   15
D'you hear this, Eadwacer?   It's our wretched whelp
the wolf bears to the woods.
Easily sundered,   what wasn't ever of a piece:
our gift together.

A Riddle

from the Exeter Book

Four wondrous things   fall through my eyes,
travelling together.   Their tracks were black,
but pale their path.   Among these planing birds
swift was strongest: swooped up through air,
dove under water.   He worked restless,
this pioneer,   pointing the journey
all four must make   over filigreed gold.

The Battle of Maldon

He told each of his levy
to drive it away,
thinking on the day's-work:
It was Offa who first
didn't intend to
His hawk, his beloved,
She flew to the wood;
Seeing this business,
wouldn't weaken in war,
Eadric also
followed him into combat,
the ravening spear.
in the time he held
short-bladed sword.
of his promise to fight
    Then Byrhtnoth began
he rode the line,
what way to stand,
asking them to carry their
shields tight on foregrip –
Once he'd arranged them
he dismounted, among
of loyalty's pick,
    On the estuary's bank
Viking messenger,
threatening. He delivered
to the English chief
    'Savage seafarers
say I'm to tell you
now: rings in return
buying off the blade-rush
than that we share battle's
No one need perish
We'd establish a truce
If you – their gallant leader –
that you can ransom
sell Vikings peace
get security for cash…

…would be broken.
to leave their horse,
then to walk further,
duty; valour-deeds.
found that his commander   5
tolerate indolence.
he let slip from his hands.
he framed himself for battle.
one knew the boy
at the weapon-taking.   10
honoured his leader,
forward with gar's-edge,
Good recompense he had
in his hands the shield,
He showed the truth   15
in front of his chief.
to guide the levy:
teaching the retinue
what place defend,
arms correctly –   20
and telling them not to fear.
into the right attitudes
the mettle of the troop,
beloved kinsmen.
stood an emissary,   25
mouthing, shouting,
the longships' message
on the opposite shore:
send me to you,
to send tribute   30
for rest. Better for you,
in booty-giving,
shock together.
if you're prosperous enough.
with a tribute of gold.   35
will agree to it –
your kith and kin,
(price they'll determine),
…call it a 'cessation'… –

then we'll take to ship
depart on the sea-paths,
    Byrhtnoth answered,
shook the keen spear-shaft,
Furious, resolute
    'D'you hear, sea-crawler,
responds? As tribute,
point-burnished venom,
all the war-gear
    'Viking messenger,
tell your people
Here, unafraid,
fully intending
Aethelred's ground,
kin and country.
will be cut down in battle.
that you should creep seawards
taking our tribute,
already onto
Our treasury's not sold
It's grim war-play
ravage of weapons
    He drew up his battle-line
All his army
But the tide kept apart
the flood still flowed,
the twined currents.
before they could marry their
                spears
Army from longships;
ranged on the riverbank,
Yet no man could cause
unless an arrow was unloosed,
    The tide went out.
a warrior host –
    Byrhtnoth then commanded
warrior named Wulfstan
the quickest of his clan,
He overtoppled
who'd boldly advanced,
With Wulfstan stood
Aelfere and Maccus –
who were determined
but to defend it

with your tall tribute,   40
and keep peace with you.'
his shield in the air,
spoke back, enraged.
flew back his reply:
how this people   45
spears they'll send you,
violence of sword-play,
you wouldn't hazard.
take a message back –
a more terrifying tale.   50
stand an earl, his army,
to defend territory –
and my own ancestors',
Craven, you heathens
Too cowardly, it seems to me, 55
without combat,
since you've travelled so far
our territory.
so softly to you.
before you get tribute: 60
will reconcile us.'
on Blackwater's banks.
stood on the eastern shore.
the two forces –
full after ebb,   65
Too long it seemed
in mortal combat.

East Saxon mettle:
arrayed for war.
any mutual hurt   70
took life as it fell.
The Viking troop –
waited, were ready.
a battle-hardened
to ward the causeway –   75
Ceola's young son.
an adversary
ventured the crossing-place.
those sternest thanes
avid, valorous pair –   80
never to turn from the ford
fiercely against its attackers

as long as they could carry
When they discovered,
death waited there
then the unwelcome guests
wheedling for access,
across the fateful causeway
    It was then that Byrhtnoth –
allowed access
The battle-ready ones
while Byrhtelm's son
yelled 'Now, now you've room:
Let warriors make war!
best knows the victor
    Then slaughter like a wolf
cruel Viking host,
bore linden shields
westwards, on banks
Byrhtnoth and his retinue,
stood against the onslaught.
shield-walls, war-hedges,
whatever it may cost.
turmoil; glory:
would wrest from their terror
Carnage cried, ravishing.
carrion-eagles.
File-hardened spears
the grimly-ground
bows were busy there;
    The battle-rush? Bitter.
fighters fell dead,
Wulfmaer, wounded,
death. Byrhtnoth's kin
his sister's son,
Recompense was given,
Edward, it was said,
with such huge power,
that the darling of the ships
His chief gave thanks
for the act, when
    Thus English thanes –
those resolute ones –
how they might gain glory,
winning reputation
among the marauding host,

weapons in combat.
when their cruel eyes saw
on that dangerous ford,   85
used guile, taunting,
asking for passage
for their foot-soldiers.
brave, but too magnanimous –
to the longships' host.   90
bent to listen
over the brawling currents
rush on, and quickly!
It's all-witting God
in this battle-place…'   95
slipped across the river:
careless of the water,
over the shining stream,
of the Blackwater.
ready to counter,   100
He urged them to make
hold them against the enemy,
And the tumult came –
a time where fate
those already doomed.   105
Ravens circled,
Chaos ruled the earth.
flew swift from hands;
gar flew also;
there board hosted edge.   110
In both armies
the furious lay still.
in warfare chose
with a bill-hook was slain –
severed, cut apart.   115
ruin dealt Vikings.
slew one of them
not withholding the stroke,
dropped dead at his feet.
to his chamberlain   120
opportunity arose.
they thought only of valour,
readily imagined
who was going to be first
with war-reddened edge   125
while ruin struck the earth.

Steadfast they stood,
of Byrhtnoth, who required
consider only their doom:
Then a hard-bitten Dane,
with his shield as defence,
He was alike countered
intended evil,
But then the sea-man let fly
so that the English lord
at the shaft with his shield;
spear tore from wound,
Byrhtnoth was maddened then:
at the cunning Viking
And Byrhtnoth was wise,
through the plunderer's neck,
searing, extinguishing
Then yet another
cut through his corselet,
through ravaged ring-mail,
went hard to the heart…
Byrhtnoth who, laughing,
the Lord of Promise

    Then some Viking *dreng*
Hurdling the space there,
through Byrhtnoth's body,
By his leader's side
a mere boy in battle.
the blood-streaked gar
(this was young Wulfmar,
threw back the fire-hardened
Its point penetrated;
who'd wounded his lord
But yet another Viking,
came towards Byrhtnoth,
rings, war-gear, clothes,
Byrhtnoth unholstered
brown-edged, blood-flecked;
But too easily
stopped him, limiting
Gold-hilted sword
no more could he grip
he could wield nothing.
Grey-haired, aged,
valiant companions –

stirred by the encouragement
that his bold fighters
among the Danes, dying.
hefting his battle-mace,   130
feinted at Byrhtnoth.
by the leader: each
enmity to the other.
a Frankish spear,
was injured; he shoved   135
the shaft shattered,
sprang out again.
with his blade he stabbed
who'd caused his wound.
re-working his spear   140
his experienced hand
his sudden attacker.
new opponent –
to the chest cavity,
so the rabid spear-tip   145
Happier there was
blessed and gave thanks to
who'd appointed the day's-work.
threw a vicious spear.
hurtling, speeding –   150
blood-line of Aethelred.
stood an unlined warrior,
Boldly he pulled out
from Byrhtnoth's side
Wulfstan's brave son),   155
havoc back again.
the perpetrator
lay dead himself.
newly armoured,
wanting to pillage   160
the wondrous-patterned sword.
his axe from its sheath –
beat out at chain-mail…
his attacker, a nothing,
the leader's arm-blow.   165
slipped groundwards then;
the mace, war-hardened;
But words remained.
he urged his troop –
to advance, regroup…   170

It wasn't for long
He looked towards the heavens:
   'May you be thanked,
for all of the joys
Now, mildest Judge,
something of good
so my soul's journey
Into your power,
may I travel in peace;
that hell and its fiends
   Hordes of heathens
struck Aelfnoth, Wulfmar,
both of those battle-friends,
died alongside him,
But some callow cowards
Odda's fine son
Godric, galloping away
(who had many-times lent
He straddled the stirrups
conduct unbecoming;
And his vile brothers
Godwin, Godwy,
running from warfare
saving their sorry skins
And many more were
They should have brought to mind
had dealt their troop,
(Offa had told him,
as men gathered
that many there spoke
feigning endurance,
   He was lost in battle –
Aelthelred's chosen.
was clear to the clan
Those war-proud thanes
fetching courage
each determined
victory in death's-moment,
Aelfric's son, Aelfwin,
still winter-young,
About valour he spoke,
'That bragging! Recall
promises in mead-cups,
about the strife to come,

he could last, standing.

Might of Peoples,
I endured in this world.
my need's pressing: 175
may you grant my spirit
to you will be safe.
Prince of Angels,
I entreat only
won't harm my soul.'   180
hacked Byrhtnoth down,
who stood by him –
who buttressed their lord,
bought death dearly.
turned from combat: 185
was the first to flee –
from his gallant chief
the lad a horse).
of his lord's own steed:
a coward's way.   190
voided the battlefield,
disregarding their duty,
to the wood's sanctuary,
in the safety of flight.
meritless, craven.   195
all the boons Byrhtnoth
all he'd done for them.
earlier that morning,
in the meeting-place,
of merit, courage,   200
that would fail at need.)
leader, protector,
That their chief lay dead
who were close by him.
went forth to die,   205
from the face of doom,
on one fate of two:
or vengeance for their chief.
urged them onward,
that yare fighter.   210
was valorous himself:
the boasts we made,
when we met feasting,
stuff about heroes…

Now we'll discover
My ancestry?
it has merit: Mercia
my grandfather
wise in counsel,
Could I myself face down
friends, relations,
and turned for home,
with his body cut apart?
he was alike my
Then he strode away,
one Viking from the many,
he spiked with his spear.
fissured, filleted. Still
his fellows and friends
Offa shouted back,
'Aelfwin's reminded
all warriors in this peril,
extinguished in the dirt.
for each one of us
of our fighters into the fray
keep carrying weapons –
pike-staff and sword...
of Odda, Godric,
Many a man thought,
gallop proud from the fight,
therefore here on the battlefield
and the shield-wall split...
that put so many
    Leofsunu, brandishing
shield, then spoke out,
'Faithfully I promise
flight's impossible.
attempting to avenge
The steadfast warriors
to reproach me with their words
that I, lordless,
went from war wretchedly.
edge and iron.'
fought furiously,
    Next Dunnere spoke,
a humble foot-soldier,
resounding, saying
'None who think vengeance

whose courage can speak.   215
All of you know that
made me, a good family;
was the great Ealhelm,
whose world was rich.
family faces,   220
if I fled combat
now my true lord lies
Body-blow to me –
lord and my kinsman.'
stirred into hatred: 225
from the maddened throng,
Spiritless the man lay,
fair Aelfwin enjoined
to the fight ('Onward!').
shaking his ash-spear: 230
all about courage –
now our prince lies dead,
Duty makes it needful
to urge still another
for as long as his force can   235
the crafted mace,
That putrid son
has gulled us all!
when they saw Byrhtnoth's mount
that the fellow *was* our lord –   240
baffled were our swordsmen
I shit on the "courage"
of our soldiers to flight!'
his linden-rimmed
responding to Offa: 245
that not one foot I'll move –
But I'll press onward,
my true lord's death.
of Sturmer shan't have cause
now my prince is killed –   250
legged it homewards,
No, it's weapons I'll take,
Full of anger he left,
forgoing escape.
his spear aloft –   255
his high voice everywhere
that each should serve Byrhtnoth:
will know how to flinch.

They want quits for their lord,
    Onward they fought,
That peasant army,
great in the gar-rush,
that they be allowed to avenge
and bring death to
Even a hostage
From a hard family
son of Ecglaf,
He never weakened
but returned a shower
now turning a shield,
Ever and again he
for the while his strength
    At the apex of the troops
still ready for a fight,
that he'd not furnish one foot
or consider retreat
The shield-wall he shattered,
until his ring-giver
among the sea-men's terror.
Atheric did likewise,
combat-keen, eager
And Sibyrht's brother...
hacked the dark shield-rim,
Shield-spine crumpled,
its battle-songs.
at one seafarer
there too Gadd's kinsman
Offa was quickly
but he'd fulfilled there all
what earlier he'd promised
that they'd both ride back
go safely home,
die, stricken with wounds,
He lay like a true
    Defence was futile.
advanced, war-maddened.
split the willing life-house.
Thurstan's godson,
slew three of them
before Wigelin's son
Terrible the encounter.
were resolute, but

not to care about life.'
were fearless for their lives.   260
compelled spear-carriers,
asked God for help –
their leader's life
their bitter enemies.
began to help them.   265
beyond the Humber, he was –
Ashferth by name.
in war-play's terror,
of continual arrows,
now tearing a man...   270
injured some opponent
with weapons lasted.
stood Edward (the Tall),
speaking rightful words
of land to flight   275
now his sovereign lay dead.
ship-men took on
was rightfully avenged
Then he, too, perished.
loyal companion,   280
in the clash of weapons.
So many others
doughty defenders.
and the corselet sang
Brave Offa struck   285
so that he sagged to earth;
groundwards plummeted.
cut down in that skirmish,
he owed to his lord –
his prize-giver: 290
from battle in one piece,
or in the sword-crush perish,
in strife's foul ditch.
retainer by his lord.
Furiously the sea-men   295
Many a spear there
Wistan too advanced,
grappled with the enemy,
in slaughter's rush,
sank in the carnage.   300
The troops in that strife
warriors perished,

worn out by wounds,
Yet all that time
those two brothers,
in words encouraged
in present peril
make use of weapons
Then battle-hardened
shaking his shield-rim,
boldly admonishing
'More hardened the intent,
courage more capable,
Here our leader lies,
bereft, a dust-corpse.
who thinks to turn
I'm an aged man,
leaving. By my leader's
next to my Chosen,
So too the eldest son
Godric, goaded them
viciously finding
Among that folk he strode,
hacking and hewing,
But that Godric was not

warfare on earth.
Oswold and Eadwold,
emboldened their fellows,   305
kin and clansmen
to press onward,
with might and main.
Byrhtwold spoke out,
the shaved ash-staff,   310
the men left there:
heart the keener,
as our clan's diminished!
lies torn from life,
Forever may he mourn   315
from this terrible place.
but *I* shan't consider
side I shall lie,
choose there to die.'
of Aethelgar,   320
into engagement, his spear
its Viking mark.
foremost of all,
until he too perished.
the gutless one who'd left…

The Wife's Lament

About my sorrowful self
my self's turmoil.
what of griefs I've gathered
new and old, but
Always I suffered
and since my lord
went over the waves' expanse,
with where, in which land
    When I set out
friendless, governed only
my man's kinsmen
secretly plotted
so that we'd live sundered,
in the most wretched manner.
    My lord ordered me
I had no friends here
few dear or close.
Then I thought I'd found
but one ill-starred,
withdrawn, whose plan
whose smile was a knife.
'shall any violence
And nothing else.' But
now ripped away
our loving friendship,
I'm forced to suffer
    They forced me to live
under the oak's branches,
Old, this earth-cave.
Dark, these valleys
riddled with hedge-spikes
a joyless place.
I think of my lord's absence.
those dear to, those disposed
while I, alone,
around this ancient grave
where I'm forced to sit
allowed to weep
need's many hardships,

this song I utter,
I can tell truly
since I grew up, both
never more than now.
exile, misery,   5
left, left his kin,
I've worried daybreak
my lord might be.
to serve, join him –
by grievous need –   10
met covertly,
to separate us two
go lonely in the world,
I was a mind, longing.
to this ailing land.   15
in this far country,
Darkened is my thinking.
a fitting husband…
aching in spirit,
implied murder,   20
'Never,' we'd said, often,
divide us – except death.
now that has changed,
as if it never had been,
and far or near   25
this feud of my Beloved.
in this forest clearing,
in an earth-barrow.
All I do's yearn.
voided among hill-tops,   30
wrapped round with briars:
Jealously, fiercely here
There are lovers on earth,
in their dear one's bed,
at first light will pace   35
under the oak's branches,
the summer-long day,
longing, exile,
since I'm never able

to still, set at rest
nor the fraught longing
    The young always
    tough in character;
    good comportment,
    what ravening cares.
    in the world's within…
it may be that my Dear One –
sits where storms hammer
lives weary in spirit,
in some desolate hall;
is mauled by sorrows,
a happier place.
lives in longing

the strife in my mind   40
fetched me from life.
    should yearn to be serious,
    so too they should have
    whatever problems may press,
    Their right to be happy   45
There, far outcast,
distant, stranded –
at cliffs in hoar-frost,
by water marooned
that my Dear Beloved   50
remembering too often
But whosoever
shall alone find grief.

The Husband's Message

Now I say this message   to sundered You:
… tree-kind.   I was their true offspring.
On me, men…   …must…
from other lands   send…
the salt currents…   …ss…   5
Often in the boat's belly…   …sought…
where my lord…   …my…
over the fathomless holm.   Here I'm now come
by keel's journey,   and care to discover
how you think of   my heart's lord in   10
the deeps of your mind.   I dare promise
great faithfulness   you'll get to find there.

Wait… Who graved this shard

      again bids me tell
you – jewelled You –   in your young, secret
heart to remember   that heart's promises,   15
mutual, spoken   in the midst of times
when you both still lived   in the lovely cities,
permitted that place   of mead and promise
to enact your love.   Need, feud drove him
from that great people,   but he impels me now   20
to urge you to cross   the ocean joyfully –
as soon as you've heard   on the hill's margin
the cuckoo, singing   sadly in the copses.
Don't let anything   delay your crossing,
revoke, defer –   No other vivid man.   25
Seek out ocean,   sea-tern's homeland.
Board any prow there   that's pointing south,
so that over the fractious currents

      you shall find your lord,
rejoin him, where he's wedded

      to waiting for you.
No wish in the world –   he witnessed to me himself –   30
is more in his mind   than that mighty God
grant the two of you,   again together,
power to distribute   to your people –
to friends, comrades –   fabulous treasures,
embossed bracelets.   Of such bounty enough   35

he has, gold-work fair...
among a foreign tribe
extensive lands...
true retainers,
...
driven and needy,
and on the locked expanse,
was exiled on the sail-paths,
twining time-currents.
has nulled his woes.
not horses, not jewels,
nor any noble treasure
O royal daughter,
About the long-ago vows
I hear S. and R.
to EA., W. and M. –
and promised to keep,
under heaven, on earth.
that vow you two made

...
a fine manor,
...
although at that time my lord...
...   40
undocked his boat,
alone, at sea,
eager to travel the
And now truly that man
There's nothing he might lack – 45
nor the hall's comforts,
of the noble earth,
if his riches are You.
you two once voiced
he supply coupled   50
an oath he declared
pledge of fidelity
And he's held it fast,
in the vanishing days.

A Charm

Against stabbing pain.
Feverfew, and the red nettle which grows in grain, and plantain.
Boil with butter.

Ravening, yes – clamouring   when they rode over the corpse;
resolute they were when   they rode over the land.
Protect yourself now   so your trouble might be cured.   5
Out, little spear...   *if it's in here.*
Under the linden-wood   he stood, the light shield,
where that bitch of a woman   brought force to mind,
where they, screaming,   hurled screaming spears...
It's another one   I want to hurl –   10
an arrow in front,   flying towards them!
Out, little spear...   *if it's in here.*
A smith sat   forging a small battle-axe...
... by iron   wounded badly.
Out, spear...   *if you're in here.*   15
Six smiths sat, forging   spears for slaughter...
Out, spear...   *Not in, spear!*
If a sliver of iron   lies in this place,
those hags' mad-work,   may it melt now!
If your skin had sheared;   if you'd been shot through
     flesh;   20

if your blood were tainted,   if your bones broken,
your limbs twisted...   your life would never
     have been touched.

Whether it were Æsir-wound;   whether elves'-wounding;
whether hags'-wound...   Now I'll help you.
This, remedy for Æsir-wound;   this, remedy for elves'-
     wounding;   25
this, remedy for hags'-wound...and help you I will!
Flee away there   to the fell's summit!
Get well! Be whole!   And may your god help you!
Pick up that axe,   put it in water...

A Riddle

from the Exeter Book

My neb was in the narrows,   beneath water,
underflowed by flood,   in fell torrents
deep-sunk, awash…   I woke in the sea,
the waves covered me,   I clung only
onto flotsam   with my fragile body.   5
I had a live spirit.   Though spawned in the clutch
of water and wood   in my wan raiment,
sometimes my trappings   turned brightest white,
air lifted me,   living, up aloft,
a breeze from a wave,   then bore me away   10
over the seals'-bath.   Say what I'm called.

Waldere (I)

'Wayland's working
for any man who's
Mimming's sharpness.
has died, blood-freaked,
Pride of Attila,
uncouple from the day,
…
that you'll undergo
the loss of your life,
summoned among peoples,
I wouldn't chide you,
though I saw you
disgraced, avoiding
any man's forcings;
saving your skin when
cut at your corselet
but continually
further and further…
that you, too noble,
surrender position
in the bray's foment.
by happy outcomes
Trust your sword's service:
granted as help-meet,
you'll humble, diminish –
these encounters
He refused this blade;
manifold ring-gifts;
he'll leave the battle
unpraised, lordless –
if he the…'

…listened intently:
won't weaken or fail
able to handle
One man after another
in battle, sword-hurt.   5
don't let your prowess ever
or courage…
Now the time has come
either of two fates:
or the long judgement   10
son of Ælfhere.
my cherished warrior,
at the supple sword-play
the violence of battle,
fleeing the ramparts,   15
the swart enemy
with cruel axes;
it was combat you sought,
Therefore fate fretted me,
wouldn't yield in battle,   20
to the rage of others
May you be favoured
in the hands of your god!
it's the most subtle of treasures
with which Guthere's boast   25
since he's manufactured
cravenly, unjustly.
fine treasure-caskets,
and now reft of both
and limp homewards   30
or perish here first,

from *Sermo Lupi ad Anglos*
(Wulfstan's address to the English)

... In this time, many on earth
are multiply blemished by the maimings of sin.
In this time
are man-slayers, kin-slayers, minister-killers and minster-
haters.

In this time
there are perjurers and murderers, meretrixes and bairn-smotherers,
and the filthy whoring of foul fornicators.
And in this time
there are spell-makers and sorceresses.
And in this time
there are plunderers, predators and preying spoliators –
and, to be brief,
a countless number of all manner of crimes and misdemeanours.
And this causes us no shame!
Rather, it should concern us that we begin atonement,
as the books teach us, and that this should be witnessed
among this wretched, vile and vice-corrupted people.
But again – much may still be called to mind, and too easily,
that would escape a mere one man's momentary consideration,
a great deal that would witness how continually wretched
things are at this time everywhere among this folk.
Urgent it is that we look, consider, nor leave the looking too long.
Therefore, and in the name of God, let us act as is necessary,
and protect, guard ourselves, as with grace we may,
else we were all to perish together...

Selections from *Beowulf*

Heorot and Grendel, ll. 64–163

Hrothgar prospered,
his warriors' honour.
readily obeyed him;
a mighty force.
commanding the making
triumphal mead-hall
mightier than menfolk
and in it, to all –
to grant, share, deal
beyond what was already
It was told widely
peoples of middle-earth
to adorn that dwelling.
dint of willingness,
stood the wonderful hall
and punning in his power,
    He broke no vow.
treasure during feasting.
high, horn-gabled –
of hostile fire.
when the blade-hatred
would wake, violent,
    Jealously the unjust one,
suffered the daylight,
a demon, each day
the noise of the hall.
poet's clear-voiced song.
told the creation
said the Almighty
eye-restful places,
set, triumphant,
for lights, to illumine
and decorated
with tree-limbs, leaves;
for quick creatures
    And so his lord's-men
most blessedly –

was given power in war,
All his retainers   65
their ranks comprised
And in his mind he weighed
of a meeting-place,
constructed by men,
had ever heard mentioned,   70
to old and young –
what God ordained
owned by right in common.
that the treasures of many
had been on merit ordered   75
And by due season,
they were done, and ready
that some wordsmith, clever
praised as 'Heorot'.
Bracelets he gave there,   80
Towering the structure –
but waiting for the huge surges
That future wasn't yet –
of broken oaths
among vicious enemies.   85
enduring darkness,
though his durance was shadows;
doomed to hear rejoicing,
There was harp-music,
Who knew, recited,   90
of earth for men,
made the landscape,
surrounded by water;
the sun and moon
land for its dwellers;   95
the dales of ground
life he also formed
of every kind.
lived in abundance,
till one, their bane,   100

a hell-creature,
He was named Grendel,
infamous reiver
waste-places, margins.
this miserable half-man,
after the Lord banished him
dreadful kindred –
deemed by the Saviour
Uncondoned, evil,
for that fell murder,
From him are descended
the monsters, the elves,
those misbegotten,
on time's traverse
    The visitor neared,
crept to the soaring walls,
were abandoned to rest
found there within
asleep, unconcerned,
they were careless.
grim and greedy,
rapacious, savage,
thirty warriors.
who's secured its prize,
seeking his lair with
    It was only at dawn,
that Grendel's cunning
and once it was confirmed,
tore at the morning.
beyond goodness now –
among sorrow's surges,
after they'd shown him
of their vicious guest.
it was, hateful, without end –
since on successive nights
committed atrocity,
of wrongdoing, evil;
    They slept afterwards
each choosing for himself
among distant rooms,
of the hall's occupant
an overt hatred.
they kept firmly
    So Grendel ruled,

began his crimes.
their wrathful guest –
who ravened the moors,
He'd remained a while,
in the no-home of monsters   105
among the bale of Cain's
the dear justice
for Abel's death.
he was exiled by God
far from humanity.   110
all sin's offspring –
orc-corpse carrion –
who contended with God
until His requital.
after night's coming,   115
saw how the Ring-Danes
after their beer-party;
the force of the troop
in a post-supper stupor;
And the creature, unhallowed, 120
gathered his durance,
then from their sleep ripped
From there, like any predator
he carried them home,
loot from the slaughter.   125
at cracked daybreak,
became common knowledge,
a foment of cries
Motionless, Hrothgar –
sat grief-stricken   130
a succour for no man
the shocking footprints
Severe hardship
hideous precedent,
anew Grendel   135
untroubled by conscience
too rapt in sin.
at a safe distance,
a separate bed
once the deadly malice   140
was unambiguous,
Evasion, escape –
to far quarters.
an inglorious

one among many.
at last, the great hall.
those troubles he endured
the Scyldings' lord –
the country of sorrows.
the children of men,
no guarded secret:
endlessly with Hrothgar,
summer and winter,
turmoil, continual…
couldn't accept from
wouldn't cease from malice,
of the company, none
for slain kinsmen
Pain – merciless,
Death's cunning shadow
alike drifted;
mist-shrouded moors,
when next, or where,

It stood empty at night   145
That lasted years:
for twelve winters,
lost in miseries,
And so it became known to
the mournful tale   150
Grendel contended
enmity endured
sick violence,
And truce? Truce he
any scion of the Danes,   155
nor settle for terms;
could expect compensation
at their slayer's hands.
remorseless – he caused.
over the adult and young   160
fouled darkness possessed
and men couldn't say
the necromancer would strike…

*

Beowulf's arrival at Heorot, ll. 301–59

The boat lay still.
It rode on its ropes,
secure, anchored.
over cheek-guards; gold-
their lives, bolstered
Fighters kindled,
they marched together
high-timbered hall,
Among mighty halls
among earth's peoples –
Its light carried
One battle-worthy
this great landmark
these travellers from afar,
edgy, careful,
'I must leave you.
and hold you in his grace,
sure journey's end.
holding watch for
The path was straight,

a roomy vessel,
Boar's crests glittered
cherished, it protected
in bright smith-fire.   305
force hastened on:
until they could glimpse it –
gold-heavy: Heorot.
it was the most fabled
and within, Hrothgar.   310
over the lands round it.
witness showed them
so they could gain the way,
then turned back to his horse,
calling over his shoulder   315
May the Lord keep you
grant you safety,
It's our shoreline I guard,
hostile intruders.'
stone-paved; admitted   320

men walking together.
hardened, hand-crafted,
sang in battle-dresses.
unthreatening in
they set down their shields –
spell-burnished rims
chose to enter,
all warrior-like.
war-devices,
ash-wood upright
Custom was honoured.
One fighter puzzled
'From where have you brought
ash-grey armour,
these stocks for strife?
Hrothgar's emissary.
so many of a force
It must be high spirits
magnanimity, courage,
He was answered by
by the Weders' chief,
resounding from his helmet:
and hearth-brothers.
And certainly I shall tell
your renowned leader –
If he so wishes,
then we'll greet his honour
Wulfgar then spoke;
winning integrity
carried his reputation:
scion of Scyldings,
tell our treasure-giver
a far-traveller
His answer I'll return
whatever the reply
    He hurried off
aged, silver-haired
strong-minded Wulfgar
capably courteous,

Their mail-shirts shone:
hoops of iron
And so they'd appear
all that war-gear
sea-weary travellers –   325
at the spar of an outbuilding;
chain-mail chiming,
Outside, their spears,
stood against a wall,
in ash-grey dawn.   330
Then came questions.
at their purpose, origin:
these embossed shield-fronts,
artfully-made helmets,
Understand that I'm   335
I've hardly seen
look so magnificent.
spur you to Hrothgar –
rather than exile's needs.'
battle's reputation,   340
whose words issued
'We're Higelac's men
Beowulf's my name.
the son of Healfdane –
the news I must.   345
your ancestral head,
in good fashion.'
he was of Wendel stock;
in both wisdom and war
'I'll acquaint Hrothgar,   350
with your self-assured request,
that you're a petitioner,
to our fabled chief.
as early as I can –
of our prince might be.'   355
to where Hrothgar sat –
among his set of men;
stood face-to-face,
with the Danish king…

*

Unferth then spoke –
who crouched at the feet
and Beowulf's bane
despised the newcomer,
His envy wouldn't allow
on middle-earth
more cared-for under heaven,
    'Are you *that* Beowulf –
who contended at swimming
foolhardy, trying
risking danger
besotted with pride?
Neither friend nor foe,
could convince you
Sorry enterprise!
plunged your hand-strokes
yawed in wave-yell,
surged with winter.
in the callous waters.
had the more power.
sea disgorged him
and he turned for home,
land of the Brondings,
their fair strongholds.
property; possessions.
by Beanstan's son
What confidence, then –
Beowulf's big repute
could I drag up
night-shadowed approach?
    Beowulf, Ecgtheow's
'My dear Unferth...
that you should speak of
so spitefully?
I, ocean-strong,
among the waves' hurling
We two, you know,
had once boasted –
green and growing –
onto the quickening sea.
We had a bare sword-blade –
which we carried swimming.

Ecglaf's offspring,
of the Scylding king –   500
unburdened his spite,
and displeased many.
any other man
to be more esteemed,
than he himself.   505
Breca's opponent,
in the sea's salt waves,
the ocean's face,
in deep water,
Dissuade you two?   510
when you fared the torrents,
of your vainglory.
The ocean you embraced,
into the pale sea-paths,
while the yellow breakers   515
Seven nights you hung
And he overcame you –
As another morning broke,
on the Raumar's sands
his ancestral turf,   520
his beloved people,
Family he had there,
His promise beat yours:
you were bested.
despite rumour's clang,   525
at battle's onset –
that you'd dare Grendel's
I expect the worst.'
offspring, then spoke:
Are you drunk, in liquor,   530
Breca's spirit and journey
It's a sure truth that
had an easier power
than...whomsoever.
way back in childhood   535
we were both then still
that we'd go, miles out,
And that we accomplished.
burnished, hand-heavy –
(It was the incursion of whales 540

we wanted to prevent.)
prised him yet from me,
subtle undertow…
Sutured together,
five nights all told,
dangerous combers,
It was coldest weather;
in darkening night,
steep-sided waves,
It was the ring-hardened
provided defence
interlocked chain-links
protecting my body.
sea-serpent I
a grim death-grip.
as the beast still writhed,
in its forehead, destroy
that lashing animal's
    There were further attacks.
by these loathsome things,
with my trusted sword –
They took no joy
those revolting beings,
at their monstrous wakes
and the next morning,
they lay swollen
slain by blade-fury,
sea-travellers would never
about what underlay their path.

God's bright beacon;
subsided. Here
wind-battered cliff-walls…
destiny will cherish
So it happened
killed nine monsters,
of a harder fight
in a night's skirmish,
of a more hard-pressed fighter.
granted me safety,
exhausted in its flood,
in surging tides.

of you, Unferth,

No wave, no tide
no puling current,
Nor would I leave him.
on that sea we swam
until a malevolent tide,   545
then drove us apart.
we were caught out there
north-griping wind,
a stricken ocean.
rigs of my corselet   550
against vicious sea-monsters –
lay, touched with gold,
One battle-mottled
seized, dragged it down;
It was granted me,   555
to bury the sword
by force of my hand
livid onrush.
Tested often
I relieved them of time   560
as was entirely fit.
in the turn of fate,
obliged to receive me
on the mere's bottom;
de-natured by swords'-play,   565
on the shoreline's sands,
so that in those buttressed fjords
afterwards think twice

Light flamed the east,
the boiling of the sea   570
I could see headlands,
If his courage is good,
its chosen warrior.
that my sword's keen edge
and never was there told   575
under the heavens' wheeling,
in ocean's scath,
Yet my power and grip
and the sea bore me,
to the Finns' homeland   580

Have I heard anyone tell
any such battle-feat,

bruited sword-bale?
no, neither of you –
performed a deed
with etched sword-blade –
nor would, were you to battle
one who harms your kin.
your bravery will be judged –
I say truly,
that Grendel would never
humiliating crimes
if your heart and valour
fierce and lasting
and yet he's discovered
hasn't learnt to dread
from those vicious victims,
extracts his toll,
to no mercy,
slays, sends to death,
of Danish spears!
Geatish courage,
will soon offer him

Even Breca never –
in the noise of battle
so dangerous   585
you think I boast overmuch? –
your brothers' slayer,
It's in hell, Unferth,
however big your brains.
son of Ecglaf,   590
have visited such grim,
on Heorot's majesty
had been as unvanquished,
as you dare allege –
he doesn't have to care!   595
lashing sword-tumult
those 'victors' the Danes!
treats all your folk
mangles where he pleases,
receiving no return   600
I'll dare show him
combat's clamour,
opposition...'

*

Beowulf and Grendel, ll. 710–824

Out of the moorland,
cursed, shunned by God,
This ravager meant
entrap them by trickery
This cloud-walker
and plain in his sight
and their gold filigree.
he'd sought Hrothgar's
but never before,
did he find harder luck
So, joy-deprived,
came to the fortress.
on the door gave way,
He broached, hostile,
intent, enraged.
the fiend tread-marked
in ire came on.
something like firelight,

falls of mist-slopes,   710
Grendel came walking.
to harm menfolk,
in the towering hall.
came to the building,
were the plated walls   715
It wasn't his first venture –
homestead before –
never afterwards
among the hall's guardians.
this journeying man   720
Forged metal hinges
as soon wrecked as touched.
hall's cavernous mouth,
Too soon afterwards
the tessellated floor,   725
In his eyes flickered
flames of hatred.

A gathering of men
band of kinsmen;
brave thanes...asleep.
Before another daybreak
each one's body from life.
fury had found them
his prey... But now
his fate, after that night,
more men-children.
Higelac's kinsman –
the surge of will,
Grendel's brutality
as his first assay
a sleeping guard,
he bit muscles,
swallowed gulps of bone.
all of the cadaver –
feet, limp fingers.
tried to seize another
to rip him from sleeping...
sat up the same moment,
held hostility
That brew of crimes
that never on middle-earth
a mightier grip
nor anywhere under heaven.
was sickened by fear;
Frit mind, shaken...
concourse with devils...
lay not in living
Then Higelac's thane
of his speech that night,
and fastened his grip.
the creature was fleeing...
However, wherever,
wished only to escape
vanish into remoteness,
were in a remorseless grasp...
to Heorot that harm
Hall-timbers dinned.
each of the men who
there was desperate terror.
filled both fighters;
resounded – miraculous

his gaze compassed:
brothers' dormitory;
His ambition laughed.   730
his due was to part
Livid, he exulted:
after their feasting,
it was no longer
to unfurnish, devour   735
Mighty eyes there –
weighed his horrible intent,
the sudden attack.
brooked no delay:
his fist enclosed   740
greedily tore him;
drank blood from veins,
Soon he'd eaten
all of it, even
He went forward, approached, 745
sane-minded man,
He reached out in turn,
sensing malice,
in a huge hammer-lock.
discovered instantly   750
had his knowledge met
from any mortal,
He was uneasy,
none sooner would flee.
Shadows he longed for,   755
But his destiny now
as in the long-ago.
thought, and worthily,
stood spear-upright
Fingers shattered there...   760
then closer came the man...
the hostile felon
unscathed, and from there
yet his vicious fingers
Grievous, the journey   765
had had to make!
Among the Danes there,
manned the stronghold,
Tearing anger
the frame of the hall   770
that its rafters stood

fury's combat,
such a fair structure;
inside and out
forged skilfully.
the gathered mead-benches
battered from their bases
or so I've hear rumoured.)
those Scylding *witan*
that their splendid hall,
could threaten to shatter,
unless fire swallowed it?
new, unfamiliar.
defending positions
were transfixed by fear,
ghoulish melodies
his song of defeat,
of hell's inmate,
of the man whose power,
at that time in
　　By no means did
intend to leave the
nor perpetuate
among any other people.
Beowulf's retinue
wherever, however,
was required to defend
As they undertook combat
resolute warriors
every side, striving
of their un-souled enemy,
foe had rendered
everywhere useless,
war-pike could ever
At that time in
his parting from life
a more wretched manner,
exiled into misery,
He once had in mind
mutilation
time's reprobate,
But now he discovered his
Higelac's kinsman,
was tightening his grip.
were a torment to each other:

that it didn't fall to earth,
but it was strengthened
with iron shackles
(Yet its furnishings,　　　　775
with their gold cladding,
while the bale played out –
Could they ever have reckoned,
with their wise counsels,
hung with antlers,　　　　780
be dishevelled by cunning –
But now fury was sound –
North Danish guards,
on the furthest wall,
hearing failure's song,　　　785
of God's enemy,
the furious lament
still held in the grip
might was strongest
this transitory world.　　　790
the men's guardian
terror-bringer alive,
that pointless life
And their ancestral swords
began to brandish:　　　　795
he who was able
his captain's life.
they couldn't know,
wanting to rain blows on
to seek the life　　　　　800
that their sin-stricken
wrought iron's blades
so that no earthly weapon,
cause him any injury.
this transitory world　　　805
had to take place in
and his maimed spirit be
the Otherworld's malice.
murder, affliction,
among men-folk –　　　　810
who contended with God.
skin was perishable:
unrequitable,
The two, while alive,
it was agony of body　　　815

Grendel suffered there.
a sudden wound-gape:
and cartilages burst.
victory was granted.
mortally wounded
his friendless dwelling,
end, and the ending
his numbered days.
had been fulfilled

In his shoulder appeared
sinews tore apart,
It was to Beowulf
And Grendel fled
to the mist-havens,   820
fearing certainty's
of all his life,
The Danes' wishes
in fury and blood.

*

The mere and Grendel's mother, ll. 1422–622

Their troop looked on
boiling with heart's-gore.
brute battle-song.
glimpsed things writhing
squirming sea-dragons
like those harmful beasts
which at dark daybreak
they're worms, snake-coils –
disaster to ships
Startled, those serpents
submerged, enraged
One Geat loosed
at a swimming creature,
from Beowulf's position.
painfully hindered,
Then barbed boar-spears
worked at waves'-edge,
drew onto the headland
strange wave-traverser:
under the eyes of men.

a lake – blood-mired,
A horn gave out
Brave foot-soldiers
among the water-thirl,   1425
whose scope was waves –
which lurk among headlands,
often deem it fit –
to wreak havoc,
on short sail-roads.   1430
like stones sank away,
by the ringing horn-note.
an arrow from afar
a swift war-dart,
The beast was slow,   1435
and perished swimming.
brutally, quickly
wound-opening malice…
their dangerous guest,
an astonishing corpse   1440

clad himself in armour,
That war-corselet,
had pledged duty
It knew how to keep
neither fierce attack
malice ever could harm
And the white helmet
which would merge with
turn through water's-moil,

Meanwhile Beowulf
careless of danger.
woven cunningly,
to explore the mere.
breath's cave uninjured;   1445
nor foe's grasping
the man wearing it.
protected his head –
the mere's soundings,
a treasured object,   1450

encircled, endowed...\
In days long ago\
a smith worked it\
with wondrous skill,\
armed it with boar-brass,\
so that afterwards\
no sword, no battle-mace\
could bite through it.\
And not the least aid to\
his legendary strength 1455\
was the blade lent him\
by Hrothgar's ambassador:\
that miraculous hilt\
was called Hrunting,\
was hugely the best\
of inherited treasures –\
sharp, iron-edged,\
shining venom-carved,\
hardened in war's-blood...\
It had never weakened yet 1460\
in anyone's grip\
if they understood its use,\
dared undergo\
danger, battle-journeys\
to enemy dwellings.\
Due was its moment:\
again it would practise\
its gift of valour.\
    Hrothgar's kinsman\
didn't care to recall, 1465\
in his cunning power,\
his putrid words –\
besotted, wine-glutted –\
when his weapon was given\
to the better swordsman.\
His baleful self\
wouldn't risk its life\
under the roiling waves.\
He lost courage,\
therefore lost respect, 1470\
the possibility of fame.\
With Beowulf it was otherwise\
after he'd prepared for\
the press of the fray.\
    Beowulf, Ecgtheow's child, chose then to speak:\
'Consider, beloved\
leader of Halfdanes,\
their guide, counsel,\
gold-protector, 1475\
in this time's readiness,\
what we two agreed:\
If in your service\
I should ever be\
parted from the living,\
then you'd be pleased to assume\
after that fatality\
a father's office.\
Be you protector\
to my troop of thanes, 1480\
close kinsmen, if\
combat claim me,\
and – beloved Hrothgar –\
to Higelac send\
those gifts of treasure\
you've graced me with.\
Then will the Geats' sovereign, son of Hrethel, 1485\
be able to see,\
discern in the legacy,\
how a great ring-giver,\
glorious in virtue,\
granted me bounty.\
And... Bold Unferth:\
this wrought way-sword\
your reputation\
gave me, havoc-edged.\
With Hrunting I 1490\
shall endure judgement,\
be juried by death.'\
Those words spoken,\
the Weders' chief\
strode off, away,\
nor waited for reply.\
The waters' whelm,\
wave-chaos, enwrapped\
a mortal swimmer.\
It was most of that day 1495

before he could fathom,

  Hundreds of half-years
the flood's expanse,
greedy, terrible.
that one of human kind
She grappled him, grabbed
with horrible claws,
but couldn't do harm.
couldn't be penetrated;
found no purchase
But at their plummet's nadir
on the corselet's cover.
No matter how brave,
wield his weapons there:
enraged sea-monsters
their sword-like tusks
teeth tearing him…
something impossible,
which no water
A vaulted roof
from falling, and fire
its pale flame-tongues
  The good warrior;
the mere's brutality.
at last he struck,
around her head
their stricken war-song.
the battle-knife's edge
could injure nothing:
in his second of need.
hand-to-hand combat,
fate-struck chain-mail…
dear-made war-trappings
  Still, resolute was
kinsman of Higelac,
He cast off his sword,
Anger left it.
strong and steel-edged.

that mighty grip.
if they think to gain
long-lasting fame,
  Then the Geat warrior
by the shoulders, sure

find lake-bottom.
she'd held, guarded
fiercely ravenous,
She could tell at once
swam through her holt. 1500
at the garb of war
hauled at him as they plummeted –
His corselet, spell-woven,
her probing nails
on the patterned chain-locks. 1505
her nails fastened
She carried him to her lair.
Beowulf could not
worm-writhing devils,
rucked around him, 1510
snagging at his armour,
In the turmoil he saw
some sort of hell,
could overwhelm or reach.
kept the rushing lake-flood 1515
flickered there within,
faint and putrid.
the witch of mud,
Finding his battle-axe
no restraint in the swing: 1520
ring-patterns sang out
But the stranger found
had no easy bite,
edge failed its man
Then suffered the hours, 1525
his helmet split,
For the first time his
left their doom doubtful.
that stern-minded
and careful of fame. 1530
with its serpentine patterns.
It lay on the ground,
But it was his own strength he'd
       trust –
So men must do
in the thresh of war 1535
nor life over-reckon.
seized Grendel's mother
in that unsure combat;

he flung her about,
she landed in dirt,
quickly quit him –
claws grabbed at him –
Even that mightiest of men,
stricken half to death,
Deadly, visitant,
the swart-edged sword...
for her only kin...
lay the supple chain-mail.
withstood the ravages
There might Ecgtheow's son
in that submerged country –
had not the wrought war-shirt
spell-bound battle-net;
all-knowing in
the heavens' Reasoner,
deemed for Beowulf...

    Among the den's debris
age-old giant-work
whose memory was honour:
but so heavy with merit
could ever have employed
and purpose there
Yet Hrothgar's man,
seized the wrapped war-hilt –
despairing, with the patterned
It buried brutally
cracked, cartilage
spilled from the spear-point.
moisture stained the edge;

    Surrounded by light,
like the holy, clear
that's the sky's candle –
hugged the wall's-edge,
hefted again his
his mind occupied
was still useful,
was to repay Grendel
he'd made to the Danes,
when he'd torn Hrothgar's
ripped them from sleeping,
fifteen fighting-men

battle-enraged, and
livid foe-woman – 1540
requited the blow –
crushed him breathless.
almost overmastered,
stumbled in weariness.
she drew her knife, 1545
For her son, vengeance –
But on his chest's axle
It saved his life,
of ripping knife-point.
early have perished, 1550
the might of the Geats –
worked its magic,
had not the spirit of God,
the numbers of war,
rightly and easily 1555
who dragged himself to his feet.
one sword endured –
whose edge hadn't aged,
a meritable weapon,
that no other man 1560
its ancient weight
in the play of battle.
unhesitating,
in wanhope struck,
sprig of war-steel... 1565
in her body; her neck
from her spine's column
She sprawled to the ground;
man exulted.
riddled with brightness – 1570
heavenly shining
he squinted at the cave,
Higelac's champion,
hard-hilted weapon,
by anger. That blade 1575
since his stern intent
for the appalling visits
no more than for the time
hearth-friends from dreams,
swallowed alive 1580
from the Danes' family.

And there were others, countless, whom he'd carried off

to his loathsome dam,
That cruel ravager
for his vicious violence:
the mangled remains –
among death's litter.
carnage in Heorot.
Two deaths it suffered
its body hewn, and

  Those havering, watchers with Hrothgar on the bank,

by supple water
dead blooms of blood
a gathering stain.
murmured together
didn't expect to see
wouldn't ever return
to our most royal...
that the pool's she-wolf
Noon came and went.
troop began to
Those heroes dispersed,
Geats continued
They wished without hope
emerge, and in the flesh...

as if an icicle burnt,
began to waste away.
it vanished altogether,
by the Father of heaven
when He who sways
Wielder of World-truth,
Yet the Geats' leader,
seeing loot and treasure
took only the monster's head
a stained bounty.
was the sword's broad blade.
killed in his den was

  Then he was swimming,
upwards, still living
Cleansed, purified
and its long coastline,
whose life had been finished

to their lake's squalor.
was requited in full
his victor saw   1585
Grendel, mortal –
Their downfall had been
He hacked at the corpse.
in that terrible blow –
its head carved off.   1590
waiting, now saw
adrift in the currents,
Grey-chinned elders
about Beowulf's merits... 1595
such a prince again...
triumphant, back
Many there alleged
had pulled him apart.
At the ness, Hrothgar's 1600
return homewards.
while the horror-stricken
to gaze at the mere.
to witness their beloved

Momentarily,   1605
Beowulf's battle-sword
A wonder, certainly:
like ice disengaged
from frost-fetters
the seasons and their times, 1610
unbinds water.
gathering booty,
littered around him,
and the maimed sword-hilt –
(Burnt and melted   1615
The blood of the one
death's corrosion.)
searching, diving
beyond the last of strife.
was that expanse of lake 1620
unpolluted by the ghost
among the fret of time.

*

The waking of the dragon, ll. 2200–309a

In later days, after the lash of battle, 2200
after Hygelac's death and Heardred's fall –
when swords turned slayers under shield-swaying
and that turbulent, blood-freaked tribe of Scylfings
sought their victories in an unsubtle time,
envious, attacking the true heir of Hereric – 2205
so it happened, so came about
that to Beowulf the broad kingdom
passed. Properly were his people ruled,
and for fifty snows – he was a fitting and wise
king, all-compasser – until a criminal One, 2210
a dragon, in doom's dark began ruling.
From his high barrow a hoard he watched,
steep place of stones. The sty's entrance
lay under, unknown to...Who knew where?
Yet someone knew. A certain man... 2215
...with his hand... from the heathen hoard...
...the age-wrought treasure that he afterwards...
...though he was reft, robbed while sleeping,
by a thief's cunning. Then the kin, the land,
its people discovered the scale of his wrath. 2220
　　The dragon's treasure wasn't disturbed with force:
who woke the dragon wasn't wilful, vicious.
Exiled, distressed, he'd struggled away
from his people's malice, men-blows, insult;
need's fugitive, a fellow of guilt, 2225
stumbling on it... Straightaway he
found that...for the visitant violence lay waiting;
yet the wretched... ...
... ...created
... danger to whoever ransacked 2230
the costly cup. Incalculable the amount
of ancient treasure in that earth-barrow.
Many years before, a mortal, unknown,
had thoughtfully hidden a huge inheritance –
dear-bought treasures of time's noble race... 2235
Death. Death destroyed them, doomed all those
old yesterdays. But one man, the last
man among clansmen, who'd remained longest,
sorrowed as he guarded those gathered treasures,
expecting he too would be allowed to look on the hoard 2240
for only the briefest time. A barrow he prepared,

equipped, occupied,
a high headland,
He bore inside
that guardian of rings –
its worthiest part –
'Now hold, O earth,
this earls' inheritance –
from you nobly.
stricken disaster,
those, my companions:
who witnessed joy.
abandoned it. And now?
Polish the plating
this glittering goblet?
The hardened helm,
shall be lustre-deprived:
bold battle-masks
and this coat of mail,
the bite of iron,
decays, posthumous;
heroes, ring out
of war-leaders.
music's intricacy;
flying there through the hall;
tramping the courtyard…
that has dismissed so many
        And so, grieving,
the one on the other.
sorrow-dazed, in time,
encroached on his heart.
force, the night-attacker,
the seeker-out
smooth-scaled hate-dragon,
who flies at dark.
fear him, and with reason.
the hoard in its earth,
guard, endlessly…
        Three hundred years
kept his eyes on
mighty in his powers,
malice there brooding,
one plated flagon,
as settlement of a feud.
had known pilfery,

a cleft by the sea –
hard to access.
the baleful treasure,
glittering plate, with gold
with words of farewell: 2245
since heroes cannot,
once, yes, obtained
But now battle-death,
has destroyed each of
perished, all of those   2250
They woke from life,
No one. Who'll brandish sword?
on this patterned flagon,
Gone, all of them.
hued with gold-work,   2255
those who prepared such
have been borne away;
knowing in conflict
bludgeon of shields,
nor shall these corselets follow   2260
everywhere in train
The winsome harp;
the mettled hawk
or horse, eagerly
Their triumph is death,   2265
of mortal kind.'
his griefs were uttered,
Afterwards he wandered,
until the tide of death
And the hoard? The old   2270
found it undefended –
of smouldering barrows,
smithied by flame-work,
Those who dwell nearby
He's forced to search out   2275
and the heathen gold
There is no greater.
this unhallowed harm
the cave of treasure,
until one man touched the   2280
bearing to his master
a peace-guarantee
Once the site of treasure
pardon was granted

to the litigants,
for the first time on
    But the worm stirred, and
he sniffed among stones,
his enemy's smell,
by stealth had disturbed
    (An undoomed man
woes and miseries
bears the Lord's favour…)
nosed out man-trace,
the one who'd troubled
shifted, enraged, through
to its outer ness.
in that burnt fastness;
intended terror;
for the rifled cup,
that someone already
ancient treasure-token.
anxiously he waited,
    The enraged raptor,
would repay his foe
the pilfered cup.
the worm set to –
of wallowing within its walls,
bright-scaled with fire…

and their lord could look   2285
that far-gathered glitter.
war's strife began:
scenting – implacable –
whose secret craft
the strength waiting…   2290
may well survive
if he's meritable,
Then, furious, the dragon
meaning to find
his terrible dreams: 2295
the shape of his cavern,
No one was there
yet his blent evil
at times he looked again
only to discover again   2300
had robbed him of the gold,
Until evening came
waited wretchedly…
rooked in his shelter,
with fire, avenge   2305
With departing day
no intention now
but to work in flames,

*

Beowulf's death, ll. 2711b–820

the rabid world-dragon
to burn, to swell:
baleful battle-heat
a poison, spreading.
moved to the wall-ramparts,
wanting to rest there,
on the ancient treasures,
held airy vaults,
Then Wiglaf, loyal
to undo the clasp
his valorous prince,
and weary to death –
Beowulf then spoke –

…Then the wound
had wrought began
soon Beowulf discovered
blooming in his body –
The prince slowly   2715
wisely and only
directing his gaze
seeing how the earth's cavern
arched stones within.
to the last, began   2720
on his clan-chief's helm –
still vivid with blood
and to wash his face.
in spite of his wound,

the number of his hurts.
that doom had closed
and their earthly joys:
into time's working.
'It's to my son I'd give
gear, war-trappings,
a guardian, to inherit
kingship's habit.
for fifty snows.
none surrounding,
dare now attack
or even threaten terror.
while I waited, trying
no murderous treachery,
oaths came to pass...
even here, weakened,
Nor can the Prince of Life
for the murder of kin,
becomes a corpse...
go, gaze on treasure
beloved Wiglaf,
is reft from its hoard
Quick now... In haste –
again on the primal
of all that glitters?
let go at last
whose zealous stewardship
Widely it was rumoured
having heard the words
then bore Beowulf –
vivid-patterned war-shirt –
As he sat there looking,
at many spoils – jewels
the gathered gold-work
an entombed miracle –
where the serpent's den,
ancestral lair,
dulled silver-work,
rusty helmets,
from fierce fighting...
envy, avarice –
may overpower a life:
And while he looked, he saw
a glorious banner

He knew full well 2725
the days of his life
all, all were gone
Mortality beckoned.
these garments, stained
as they were granted me – 2730
as I inherited
This clan I cherished
No fellow-ruler –
none anywhere –
my troops in their realm, 2735
Time happened here
to wield power well –
nor too many wrongful
Perhaps I'm owed those joys
become wound-mortal. 2740
reproach me, ever,
even as my mortal body
Quickly, this moment –
under its grey vaulting,
now the livid serpent 2745
and riddled with death.
Might I hold my eyes
gold, sense the power
Easier then to
of the glimmer of life 2750
I've preserved so long.'
that Wihstan's son,
of his wounded chief,
still in his battle-armour,
to the vault's entrance. 2755
lost in triumph,
from many a tribe,
glistering the earth-floor,
his eyes also lit
the dawn-flyer's 2760
was loaded with flagons,
dented armour,
rings, bracelets ripped
(Thus fury's greed –
easily and everywhere 2765
let that be heeded.)
aloft over the hoard
beautifully crafted,

awesome, intricate. By its ambient light
he could see further furnishings, and further, 2770
see other art-works... Sword-edge had already
taken the serpent, of whom no trace here remained.
Then – so it's told – the treasure in the barrow,
ranked antiquity, was rifled by our man,
who as the whim took him stuffed wine-cups and dishes 2775
into his bulging clothes. Even the banner he took,
brightest of symbols. Beowulf's sword-blade,
iron-work of old, had ended the life
of the one who, in aeons of winter,
had been the treasures' guardian, who – turbulent with fire – 2780
had flown darkness, dealt hatred's heat,
cruelty and murder, on account of the hoard.
Keen to flee, our furtive messenger,
but urged on alike by curiosity and fear...
And keen to return, encountering his lord – 2785
Beowulf, deprived of power, and sick –
in the place he'd left not long before.
With treasure still in his stricken fingers
he saw his own leader ailing, battle-bloodied,
his life closing. He laved him, splashed 2790
his face with liquid, until a final word
could break through the pain. Beowulf then spoke,
while looking at the gold, last words of grief:
'For these treasures I thank *the Thinker of All,*
Lord of Miracles, *with my mouth give praise* 2795
to the greatest Prince *for the good I see,*
been allowed to acquire *for my kin and clan,*
merited to gaze on *in the minute of death.*
Of the hoard, I urge – *one ultimate command*
in this last of life – *that it be left for use* 2800
as the clan need it. *I can't endure.*
I bid also *that a barrow be made –*
renowned, fire-bright, *a neb by the sea,*
a memorial *for my people*
atop the high cliff's face *at Hronesness,* 2805
so that afterwards *to all sea-travellers*
scanning in nail-ships *the nipping tideways*
it shall bear the name *of Beowulf's hill.'*
He took from his neck a torc of gold,
that grave-skilled prince, gave it to Wiglaf, 2810
his good young friend, and his gold helmet,
armour and bracelet, with 'use them well'.

'Last inheritor of long kinship,
of our Waegmundings... World's-fate has lured
my valorous clan in their virtues and powers   2815
to judgement in death. I'm due to follow.'
It was the last utterance, old one's heart-thought,
final leave-taking before fire's mettling,
searing ravages. Soul reft away,
found a less brutal and a better justice.   2820

*

The end, ll. 3137–82

The people of the Geats then prepared for him
a fitting and proper funeral barrow
hung with helmets, hued with battle-shields,
with bright corselets, just as he'd requested.   3140
In its midst they laid their mighty prince,
lamenting him, their beloved lord and protector.
Grieving warriors began to kindle
the pyre, built huge on the high headland.
Smoke climbed and scattered as swart wood caught   3145
in a crackle of flame, whose call mingled
with their tide of cries – a tumult, dying
only when his body's core broke, fire-eaten.
That death they grieved with dirges, sorrow,
one death-lay sung by a woman, who...   3150
... with hair bound up...
sang grief's concern, whose song expressed
her fear that time would fill with terror –
vicious invasion, vile kidnap's killing,
humiliation... Heaven swallowed the smoke.   3155
Then those stricken people constructed a place
on the headland's heel – high-sheltered, broad,
visible to the horizon, to those viking seas.
Ten days they built this beacon, symbol
of their lord's courage. Round what was left of ashes   3160
they built a wall, as well and splendidly
as their cleverest of men could conceive it.
Into the mound they carried the collars and jewels –
all the adornments which envious hands
had once stolen from the wondrous hoard.   3165
They let earth hold those ancient treasures,
left gold to the ground, where again it rests,
useless, unprofitable, as once before.

Twelve warriors rode around the mound.
Known for bravery, of noble descent, 3170
they would claim and name their numberless griefs,
utter in memory an elegy for their king.
Stewardship they praised; his strength and valour;
they mourned and assessed his many virtues.
Fitting it is that his fellows should praise 3175
a man's memory and merits with love
once his spirit's been fetched from its frame of life.
And so they lamented, these men of the Geats –
companions, a brotherhood – the passing of their lord.
They said that of all earthly rulers 3180
he'd been the mildest man, and the most gentle,
kindest to his clansmen – and couth in fame.

A Riddle

Lately I was abandoned,
my father and mother –
no age yet within.
courteous kinswoman,
brooded to protect me,
as honourably
Call it destiny.
grew ample with life
Ever harder my 'mother'
until I grew up, thriving,
on further travels.
meaningless offspring,

left for dead by
no force of life,
Then one, cognate,
covered, sheltered me,
tucked me into garments   5
as she would her own children.
Under that dunnage I
among my un-relatives.
had to feed me
was able to set out   10
She'd fewer of her own beloved,
more I was nurtured.

Durham

This city's famous throughout far Britain.
It's strung to the steep, a stone fastness
walled round with rocks; and Wear – enclosed,
river's rushing torrent – is riven, teeming
with many a fish-brood in the moil of currents. 5
A great wood-stretch has grown up there.
Wild animals live in that wide of forest,
and numberless beasts in the neck of dales.
Well-known to men that in the meritable town
are placed the remains of pious Cuthbert 10
and the virtuous head of the heaven-sent king
Oswald, England's guard, and Aidan the bishop,
and old nobility – Eadberch and Eadfrith.
There also interred are Athelwold the bishop,
Bede – of book-repute – and Boisil the abbott, 15
who instructed the chaste stripling Cuthbert
to reciprocal pleasure of pupil and teacher.
Buried in the minster by the much-blessed saint
are countless relics, which cause miracles
unnumbered to occur, as is known from writ, 20
while there the reeve of God waits for resurrection.

The Ruin

A miracle, these walls,
were the shattered buildings,
The roofs are wrecked,
plundered the bar-gate.
gables gaping –
eaten out by age.
masons, architects.
in hard ground's clutch.
have passed since then,
greying, red-stained
successive kingdoms,
Walls' curve declines...
...rent...penetrated...
and grimly ground...
...shone...
...old monument,
...g...
Mind lit with promise,
could build a curve,
foundations together
Then bright were the rooms,
multiply-gabled,
halls full of mead
till terror, that is time,
Plague, slaughter came,
The viciousness of death
Their bastions withered
their city decayed,
its armies became dust.
whose red-curved roof
a garrison of decline.
a pile of rubble.
glad, gold-adorned,
preening in wine-flush,
It was treasure they saw –
riches, power,
the airy breadth
Stone houses stood;
a whelm of heat,

though marred by time
shaken the giant-works.
ruined are the towers,
Plaster in frost-grip,
collapsed, a gash   5
Earth's-grip has seized
They're dismissed, perished
Hundreds of generations
while the place endured –
under gathering lichen –   10
sung at by storms.
...crumbles still the...
...
...
the...   15
ancient work...
bracelet, mud-encrusted.
and swift-purposed,
bound the determined
by dint of iron.   20
the bath-houses,
man-noise within,
and human pleasures –
took all away.
days of pestilence.   25
touched valiant men.
into waste places,
its kindlers perished,
Desolate, therefore, these strongholds,
is ravaged, its tiles   30
It's merely ruined ground,
Promising fighting-men,
glittering in armour,
moved proud, once, in trappings.
silver, gem-stones,   35
wrought stones of earth,
of a beautiful city.
stream cast a current,
where a wall compassed

its bright ambit.
a central warmth,
From there a gout of...
over the grey stonework,
und...
in circular pools.
...
Whenever...
...
how the...

Baths were placed there,   40
snug, convenient.
...
gushed warm currents
...
The pouring streams   45
into the bathing-place.
...
it's a royal custom,
...city...

Selected Manuscripts and Editions

The notes below indicate some of the scholarly editions I used during the process of translating. Poems not listed here, such as many of the riddles, originally appear in the manuscript known as the Exeter Book and feature in many different scholarly contexts, notably student textbooks such as Mitchell, Bruce and Fred C. Robinson. 1992. *A Guide to Old English* (5th edition. Oxford: Blackwell), which I have also, and gratefully, consulted during the construction of some of the new poems.

The Wanderer
Manuscript the Exeter Book.
Edition Dunning, T.P. and A.J. Bliss, eds. 1969. *The Wanderer*. London: Methuen.

Deor
Manuscript the Exeter Book.
Text Hamer, Richard. 1970. *A Choice of Anglo-Saxon Verse*. London: Faber and Faber.

The Seafarer
Manuscript the Exeter Book.
Edition Gordon, I., ed. 1979. *The Seafarer*. Manchester: Manchester University Press.

The Dream of the Rood
Manuscript the Vercelli Book.
Edition Swanton, Michael. ed., 1970. *The Dream of the Rood*. Manchester: Manchester University Press.

Bede's Death Song and **Cædmon's Hymn**
Edition Sweet, Henry. 1967. *Sweet's Anglo-Saxon Reader*. Revised edition, ed. Dorothy Whitelock. Oxford: Clarendon Press.

The Fight at Finnsburg
Edition Klaeber, F. 1950. *Beowulf, and the Fight at Finnsburg*. 3rd edition. Lexington, Mass.: D.C. Heath.

Charm ('Against bee-swarm')
Manuscript Corpus Christi College, Cambridge, MS41.

Edition Sweet, Henry. 1967. *Sweet's Anglo-Saxon Reader*. Revised edition, ed. Dorothy Whitelock. Oxford: Clarendon Press.

The Battle of Maldon
Manuscript British Museum Otho A xii, known as the Cotton manuscript. (It consists of charred fragments of the original manuscript which had been in the collection of the Cotton Library in the seventeenth century.) On the history of the manuscript, including the history of how it was transcribed, see Gordon (below), pp. 30–7.
Edition Gordon, E.V., ed. 1937. *The Battle of Maldon*. London: Methuen.

The Wife's Lament and The Husband's Message
Manuscript the Exeter Book.
Edition R.F. Leslie, ed. 1961. *Three Old English Elegies*. Manchester: Manchester University Press.

Charm ('Against stabbing pain')
Manuscript Harley MS. 585 (early eleventh century).
Edition Sweet, Henry. 1967. *Sweet's Anglo-Saxon Reader*. Revised edition, ed. Dorothy Whitelock. Oxford: Clarendon Press.

Waldere
Manuscript Two fragments of text on vellum. Royal Library, Copenhagen.
Edition Zettersten, Arne, ed. 1979. *Waldere*. New York: Barnes & Noble/ Manchester University Press.

Zettersten notes that 'Certain parts of *Waldere* can be considered obscure... The second fragment is...difficult to interpret' (p. 4). I have translated only the first fragment, which seems to be spoken by Hildegyth (Hiltgunt in the tenth century Latin analogue of the 'Walter story') to Waldere (Waltharius), encouraging him to fight with the miraculous sword, Mimming, against Guthere (Guntharius). What interests me about this fragment is the keen awareness shown by the speaker of the converse side of courage. That awareness also permeates e.g. 'Maldon', and much of *Beowulf.*

Sermo Lupi ad Anglos
Manuscript Cotton MS. Nero A.1, British Museum. There are three extant versions of the sermon, of which the Cotton text (early eleventh century) is both the longest and possibly the most authentic, since it contains entries in 'what is probably [Wulfstan's] own hand' (Sweet's *Reader*, p. 85).

Edition Sweet, Henry. 1967. *Sweet's Anglo-Saxon Reader*. Revised edition, ed.
Dorothy Whitelock. Oxford: Clarendon Press. The reader will find lines 159–75 of the *Reader* give one underlying text of the present version.

Like his contemporary Ælfric, Wulfstan (Archbishop of York, 1002–23) sometimes wrote prose of a distinctly rhythmical character. His most famous work, 'Sermo Lupi ad Anglos' (1014), whose title puns on his own name, is a good example of a sort of 'semi-verse' whose chief structural unit, clearly intended for pulpit declamation, is often a two-stress breath-group. Such breath-groups lack the intricate internal structuring, and strict closures, of purely poetic half-lines, but nevertheless they are rhetorically most effective. I have translated the chosen excerpt more than usually freely (and have of course re-lineated it so as to point its structural contours, as these appear to me). I have included it not only to give the reader some aural notion of Wulfstan in full cry, as it were (and he rather terrifies me), but also to emphasise the fact that in Old English, as in present-day English, 'poetry' and 'prose' are by no means wholly discrete types of either the creation or the experience of verbal art.

Beowulf

Manuscript MS. British Museum Cotton Vitellius A. XV.
Editions Klaeber, F. 1950. *Beowulf, and the Fight at Finnsburg*. 3rd edition. Lexington, Mass.: D.C. Heath.
Wrenn, C.L. 1973. *Beowulf, with the Finnesburg Fragment*. 3rd edition, revised by W.F. Bolton. London: Harrap.

Line references are to the Klaeber edition.

Durham

Manuscript 'Until recently, the late Old English poem *Durham* was known to have been copied in two manuscripts of the twelfth century: Cambridge, University Library, Ff. 1. 27 (C) and London, British Library, Cotton Vitellius D. xx (V). C has been transcribed frequently and serves as the basis for Elliott Van Kirk Dobbie's standard edition of the poem in the Anglo-Saxon Poetic Records. V was almost completely destroyed in the Cottonian fire of 1731. Its version is known to us solely from George Hickes's 1705 edition (H)' (www.journals.cambridge.org).
Edition www.brindin.com/poanodur.htm, with facing translation by Louis J. Rodrigues. My translation differs in several details.

'Durham' is often cited as the last poem to be composed and written in the characteristic Old English verse style. As the quote above indicates, its earliest and most reliable manuscript dates from the early twelfth century.

The Ruin
Manuscript the Exeter Book.
Edition R.F. Leslie, ed. 1961. *Three Old English Elegies*. Manchester: Manchester University Press.

Probable Solutions to Riddles

Fyfield*Books*

Two millennia of essential classics

The extensive Fyfield*Books* list includes

John Lyly *Selected Prose and Dramatic Work*
edited by Leah Scragg

Ben Jonson *Epigrams and The Forest*
edited by Richard Dutton

Giacomo Leopardi *The Canti*
with a selection of his prose
translated by J.G. Nichols

Stéphane Mallarmé *For Anatole's Tomb*
in French and English
translated by Patrick McGuinness

Andrew Marvell *Selected Poems*
edited by Bill Hutchings

Charlotte Mew *Collected Poems and Selected Prose*
edited by Val Warner

Michelangelo *Sonnets*
translated by Elizabeth Jennings, introduction by Michael Ayrton

William Morris *Selected Poems*
edited by Peter Faulkner

John Henry Newman *Selected Writings to 1845*
edited by Albert Radcliffe

Ovid *Amores*
translated by Tom Bishop

Fernando Pessoa *A Centenary Pessoa*
edited by Eugenio Lisboa and L.C. Taylor, introduction by Octavio Paz

Petrarch *Canzoniere*
translated by J.G. Nichols

Edgar Allan Poe *Poems and Essays on Poetry*
edited by C.H. Sisson

Restoration Bawdy
edited by John Adlard

Rainer Maria Rilke *Sonnets to Orpheus and Letters to a Young Poet*
translated by Stephen Cohn

Christina Rossetti *Selected Poems*
edited by C.H. Sisson

Dante Gabriel Rossetti *Selected Poems and Translations*
edited by Clive Wilmer

Sir Walter Scott *Selected Poems*
edited by James Reed

Sir Philip Sidney *Selected Writings*
edited by Richard Dutton

John Skelton *Selected Poems*
edited by Gerald Hammond

Charlotte Smith *Selected Poems*
edited by Judith Willson

Henry Howard, Earl of Surrey *Selected Poems*
edited by Dennis Keene

Algernon Charles Swinburne *Selected Poems*
edited by L.M. Findlay

Arthur Symons *Selected Writings*
edited by Roger Holdsworth

William Tyndale *Selected Writings*
edited by David Daniell

Oscar Wilde *Selected Poems*
edited by Malcolm Hicks

William Wordsworth *The Earliest Poems* edited by Duncan Wu

Sir Thomas Wyatt *Selected Poems*
edited by Hardiman Scott

For more information, including a full list of Fyfield*Books* and a contents list for each title, and details of how to order the books, visit the Carcanet website at www.carcanet.co.uk or email info@carcanet.co.uk